Eddie Lakeman mending nets on East Quay, Mevagissey c.1960

Eddie & Archie in relaxed mood, Mevagissey c.1935

EARLY TIDE

A Mevagissey Childhood

MARY LAKEMAN

CORNISH HILLSIDE PUBLICATIONS

First published in 1978 by
WILLIAM KIMBER & CO. LIMITED
London SW1H 9AE

This edition published 2003 by
CORNISH HILLSIDE PUBLICATIONS
St Austell, Cornwall

Reproduced and bound in Great Britain
by Short Run Press Limited
Exeter, Devon

ISBN 1 900 147 319

Contents

List of Illustrations

Foreword

Passing by a carpet shop in Falmouth recently, I caught sight of a hearthrug into the centre of which had been woven a picture of my grandfather's house in Mevagissey, the one with the door in the roof. Could he have seen it, what sardonic comment Tom Pollard would have made!

Sixty years fell away from me, and I sat in the window of that room overlooking the Inner Harbour watching and waiting, listening and wondering while Mother and her father conversed.

All the world comes to Mevagissey now. In our youth visitors stood out quite distinctly from the native population, a few strangers, Dr Grier's interesting looking friends, the odd ecclesiastics, and Bohemians, all with a slightly surprised look on their faces.

Today natives are outnumbered by immigrants and both obliterated for half the year by tourists. So much has everything changed we have to share our memories in order to convince ourselves that they are real.

Snug and compact, without extraneous estates, or untidy fringes of intrusive dwellings, our village encrusted the valley's end, a rare jewel adorning the meeting place of land and sea. We watched the sun rise in the Channel and set in the woods and knew that we were favoured mortals.

Looking back I saw fragments of that time emerge, multiply and combine to make a whole triumphant over time and change. Diverse characters, long since dead, began to surround those of our own household and a lost community reappeared. I recognised their faces, heard their voices, and greeted them as they moved about the streets and quays. Re-united, and levelled so to speak in time, with laughter and with tears, we pondered anew the mystery of life and death.

Acknowledgements

Five remaining brothers and sisters have jogged my memories and supplied their own.

Peter Markey read each instalment as it came up, went down the road laughing and brought me his sketches.

Heather Robinson gathered up the sheets and took them to Heather Potts who, confined always to the house, typed each chapter with speed.

Jack Dunn gladly gave me his own account of Granfer Johns, otherwise Cap'n Eckey, and John Barron that of his uncle. Gladys Barron (née Hicks) talked to me throughout an afternoon about Hicks's bakehouse, the boys, and the shop, and Margaret Hicks gave me photographs.

My old and best-loved pupil Sara Short (née Mitchell) brought me the address writ large, of William Kimber.

It is by courtesy of the latter, assisted by Amy Howlett, that I now pass my story back in print to those who helped and encouraged me.

MARY LAKEMAN

This edition of *Early Tide* in 2003 has been printed as a tribute to my aunt the author who has always been held in high regard by the Lakeman family. We are proud that the book has helped to tell of old Mevagissey and is appreciated by so many. I would like to thank Charles Thurlow of Cornish Hillside Publications for his work in re-publishing *Early Tide*. Some additional photographic illustrations from my own collection have been included in this edition. The cover is based on an original painting by Chris Hardman of St Keverne

ANDREW LAKEMAN
Portmellon
2003

I

The Community

Mevagissey society, about two thousand strong, was almost completely working class, overlaid with a thin professional topping. Drs Grier and Walker were enlightened men of integrity, and the old school master Mr Bennett a highly intelligent man of liberal persuasion. A few clerics adapted to the native population and served them well. We never seemed to attract enough resident artists to form a separate colony as did St Ives. The North Coast has a glamour with appeal less subtle than ours.

Up the valley at Heligan House, Squire Tremayne lived out his time, a neutral rather remote figure. A few country folk may have stood cap-in-hand and touched forelocks but squires never ruled the tempestuous seas, nor those who sailed upon them. Mercifully we hadn't to pay for protection and benefits they couldn't supply.

When in 1929 at eighteen I left home, I had only the sketchiest knowledge of hierarchical systems, and class barriers. Alas! the awakening was a rude one. I had entered a battlefield whereupon the impending slump was once more to bring great armies of innocents to their knees.

Growing up in isolation we knew nothing of subservience or patronage, being versed from the beginning in a sturdy independence and respect for our fellow creatures as individuals. I see now that it was a strange mixture of humility and audacity that our training engendered, safe enough when practised at home, but useless abroad where humility looks like weakness, and audacity bad form.

Families in general were big. We were eight children and this was not unusual. Poverty abject and grinding had been the lot of our parents in the decade immediately before I, the seventh child, was born in 1911.

Painfully they emerged from want during World War I and in the twenties. Fear of want is not easily exorcised. Once experienced, its shadow haunts those who have suffered it to the end, giving rise to sacrifice out of all proportion to actual need.

I do not remember any talk from my forbears of their distress, but discovered much in later years. They were stoical throughout, more grateful always for relief than resentful of destitution. Survival was regarded as a blessing rather than a right, and material comfort something to be earned daily by plenty of hard work. Work indeed was the gospel. One great blessing was gratuitous. It hadn't to be earned: it never ran out. Everybody's heritage, it was provided free, the beauty of our environment which took possession of us early. Wounds healed in the warm sun, and there was refreshment in the brilliance of sea and sky. The earth was fragrant and fertile, and the air fresh and sweet.

The life of the community was bound up almost entirely with that of the harbour and its fleet of luggers, as many as eighty, which in serried ranks filled it completely when they all rode at their moorings. Each one was like a living creature, an extension of the character of its owner, all the shapes significantly different. Their names were always on our lips, *Sunstar, Pride of the West, Diligence, Vesta, Vera, Quest, Snowdrop, Perseverance, Fairy, Emblem, Christabel, Foam, Liberty, White Heather, Westward* and the *Ibis,* my father's boat.

This is what Samuel Dunn wrote in 1838:

> Trained to fishing almost from their infancy the natives are considered the first fishermen of Cornwall. Active, enterprising and fearless, they pursue their employment with unremitting ardour and by a kind of instinctive discernment procure a reward for their superior alertness and toil.

The rhythms of the seasons, the uncertainties of the weather, the state of the tides, the look of the sky, the 'likes' in the bay, the intuitions of the crew, or perhaps of a particular one of them, determined all else.

The whole life hinged on the family lugger, everything subordinated to its movements, its departure and returns, and domestic routine for fishermen's families took on a shape as diverse, compelling, and inescapable as the elements themselves. I find myself still looking at the sky with narrowed eyes as I so often saw our menfolk doing and working sporadically and swiftly like them. Emergencies were sudden, danger always round the corner, opportunity fleeting and calling quickly to be grasped. Almost everything was unexpected, and disappointment an unknown word in the context of fortune's vagaries.

Our boat, the old *Ibis. FY 91*, named so by Granfer Lakeman, was built by Willie Frazier in his yard on the inner side of the Watch House. A model of her appears in the Mevagissey Museum; a splendid little craft, she reflected the expertise of the Fraziers, and did them credit throughout those decades both before and after engines became common.

Her successor of the same name *FY 119*, was the work of Percy Mitchell in his yard at Portmellon and into it went all Percy's youthful enthusiasm, industry, pride in good workmanship, and extraordinary skill. She was 42ft overall, bigger than the average, her frame of oak and pitchpine, the six feet tall wheelhouse having a bow front with two windows and a teak top. She was equipped with two diesel engines and her sails made by Martin Chesterfield in his workshop on the quay, part of the premises now taken over by Kelly's as a restaurant.

The cabin with bunks and lockers provided accommodation for five. A 'smooth bench ran round the little 'house' and there was a coal stove with a chimney. Clean and shining, with the fire going, it was a good place in which to take refuge.

The changing seasons sent the luggers up Channel as far as Bigbury Bay and the Bolt Head, and down beyond Land's End between Wolf Rock and the Scillies. I heard of Bishop Rock, the Longships, Manacles, Rame Head and Start Point long before I discovered their whereabouts, or particular significance.

The year began with long lining, which with the advent of engines evolved during the twenties, coming to demand a line as much as eight miles in length and baited with six thousand hooks instead of the original thousand. Distances travelled increased simultaneously, and twenty miles became thirty, forty, fifty or more. The coast was left well behind, for the line was shot in mid-channel in deep waters. The catch included skate, ray, cod, ling and turbot, and each trip took at least twenty-four hours.

Often, and especially in the early part of the year the boats encountered heavy storms. Difficulties arose, the line would 'foul' and sometimes get lost altogether, and long delays coincided with fierce gales. Baiting up, shooting, hauling, clearing the line, getting back, landing, washing down, and taking in oil for the next trip amounted to a herculean task, which left the crew fatigued in every muscle of their bodies. They trudged up the hill, their great boots burdensome, too tired almost as they appeared at the door to say Hullo.

Summer spelt pilchards, and the fleet of nets, already repaired and barked went aboard. As the season progressed the whole fleet headed westwards, for the richest pilchard grounds stretched between Land's End and the Scillies. They put into Newlyn and stayed there throughout the week coming home by train and bus on Saturdays, and leaving again on Monday mornings, bags packed with fresh food, clean overalls and jerseys. It was an exciting season and a lovely sight to see a lugger loaded with fish coming slowly into her own harbour and tying up at the quayside where an eager crowd had collected to gaze down at the sparkling catch. Two last (twenty thousand) very good.

The wide doors of the fish stores, Robins's, Pawlyn's and Edwards's, were thrown wide open, and baskets and boxes of fish swung on to the lorries while the men shouted and the gulls cried. From the top windows of our house we would be on the look-out for the return of the *Ibis* and when she was well down in the water knew there was a big catch. Mother and Dollie filled baskets with food, and made hot sweet tea in big jugs. We ran down to the quayside and left it all there, for the boys to pick up, exchanging only a nod and a smile. It was not the thing for women-folk to hang about and ask questions or evince interest in the catch. This was a man's world, and we were practised at being unobtrusive at such times. Often I think the visitors know much more about it all in a superficial sort of way than I do myself.

Coming home, first one then another, they spoke little dealing in understatements about storms and size of catches. Fortune had always to be placated. Who better than fishermen to know how capricious she can be? Who more aware of nature's vagaries, her indifference to the designs and desires of puny mortals? Ah! it was good to be home, but good always to go out again. The unpredictable begot hope, disappointment defiance.

The pilchard season was over by the end of September and dogging began. The fishbuyers' men dealt with the 'dogs' as they were landed, a great wall of fish. There was scarcely room to pass by.

Stout poles with a hook at eye-level were erected on the quay and tables stood near by. Boys got the fish to the tables where they were cleaned and then passed to the skinners. The 'dog' went on the hook and in one quick movement off came its skin. Then it went on to another table to be cut up and transformed into pink salmon, raw material for fish and chip shops.

Swift, unerring and sure, with complete co-ordination of hand and eye, those men had time by the scruff of the neck, shaking achievement out of it in the manner of perfect machines. As years went by the scene drew many spectators fascinated by so novel a performance, and the unheeding actors were further stimulated by an admiring audience.

Offal was thrown over the quay at the lighthouse, and the crowd of gulls screaming and diving became so dense as verily to blot out sea and sky.

Finally came the herring season which began in November. The cold air filled up with expectation. A time of challenge, yet another venture into the unknown. This time they were off to Plymouth and Bigbury Bay and at weekends the train brought them down the line to St Austell. We heard rumours, sometime ill-founded, of large catches, and had to 'wait and see' as Mr Asquith used to say.

It would take a hundred lifetimes to fulfil the hopes, allay the fears, contain the delight, and achieve the ambitions of those swift-moving days, those few packed years before disease and death struck. So many must remember the deceiving quality of such periods which at the time seems to arrest us in eternal youth.

Christmas intervened and the boat came home. Father brought a whole Dutch cheese from Plymouth, and once Marj had a doll dressed in yellow satin which she called Ethel after our neighbour Mrs Peters, the policeman's wife. The boys would tell us about the Salvation Army House on the Barbican where they were welcomed on stormy evenings to talk, drink tea, and eat sandwiches. There was a particularly benevolent brigadier with whom Father enjoyed conversation about social problems.

Other varieties of fishing there were, practised by special or smaller boats. Seine-boats, long and flat, shot seines (round trawls) in shallow water and left them to fill up with mackerel, returning later to collect the catch.

Spilter boats shot lines, thinner and with smaller hooks then long-lines, which caught whiting and pollock. Big boats went spiltering too.

Crabbers dropped crab-points in the right places for crabs, but not always for propellers which often got tangled up in them. The disentangling was no job for the impatient. Gorran Haven had the real crabbing community and if a Mevagissey man married a Gorran girl, he almost always had to emigrate to Gorran 'ooen'.

Some of the industry in the village directly served the fishing fleet. Mr Way had net machines at the bottom of a side street where the garage now stands opposite the railings leading to Elm Terrace. Street is the wrong word. It was a sawdusty lane, with very old rickety buildings down one side, carpenters' shops (Willie Body's), and fishermen's lofts. The Overs, Guy and Willie had their stone-mason's premises there too. The building was little more than a hut, but with great artistry, and no business acumen, they achieved excellence therein. Working gently or in gusts like the wind, they matched the rhythms of their labour to those of the songs they sang. Dick has told me of how the singing would float across to the loft, where almost opposite and with door left open, he sat listening while mending the nets.

Willie Over was always called for by Mrs Blamey, Lucy, when a dinner fell down at the back of her oven. The fire was allowed to go out, and the bakehouse shut for a day. Willie, fortified by a drink crawled into the oven to retrieve the obstructing dish, and each time would say, 'This is the last time Lucy, never again,' to which Lucy would reply, 'Oh no Willie, it isn't, you'll come when I call for you. You know very well you'll have to.'

The home of the net machines was at the bottom of the lane just round the corner from Hicks's bakehouse near the river. I loved the thin curly silken shavings and the sawdust that accumulated in heaps in that lane, and sometimes was bold enough to climb the shaky ladder, and peer into the tarry interior of father's loft, where little heaps of cables lay about on the uneven floor.

Then you could go down and watch the girls, jumping on and off the machines. I remember seeing Myrtle and Ada, Mr Way's daughters, in their long skirts, their hair swept up on their heads, and the nets growing like a curtain between the rollers. It was fascinating. You found yourself jumping on and off with them, out in the lane giving a little simultaneous hop.

Martin Chesterfield made strong sails for the boats, and well built himself, glided along the quays with a movement of a sailing ship, covering the ground quickly and showing no sign of haste. Master of his job and of situations in general, he had no need to look harassed.

It was Martin who made and embroidered a beautiful pulpit cloth for our old Methodist Fore Street Chapel; it is still in use in the River Street building.

He did look handsome on Sundays in his best navy suit with gold guard slung across his chest, and he was popular with everyone. Unambitious, the Chesterfields excited no envy, a blessed state which the gods would do well to dispense more freely.

Up beneath the Coast Guard Station above Battery Terrace

was the Rope Walk, overgrown now with brambles, where, when we were young, John James Robins made his beautiful golden ropes stretched out on the bare earth between the low green hedges. You could walk along there if work wasn't going on.

John James made hawsers for schooners and for the coal vessels at Pentewan and Charlestown. They went away piled up on a cart. He also farmed out pig nets and I remember Father making them on winter evenings using a brown shining breeding needle with a church window eye.

Then there was the Bark House in River Street attached to Sam Furse's shop. It is filled now with picture postcards.

Barking is the cleaning and curing of nets, a very important operation. The Bark House was run by Martha, Sam's mother, who had organising power and drive. She possessed the potential of a Prime Minister, having an eye for a situation in toto. She it was who got up very early and lit the furnaces ready for the barking. There were three furnaces, and three troughs and it took a hundred gallons of water to bark a fleet of nets. The taps had canvas wrapped round them.

New white nets had to be cured, and used nets washed and re-dipped, about every six weeks during the season. They used Burma Cutch in a basket which hung in the water. Then the nets were put down in a ten-gallon barrel of tar. Drained overnight, next morning they were taken on a hand-cart to the quay and spread on the harbour wall to dry.

Four men in yellow oilskins and sea boots worked like demons in the barkhouse. The place filled up with steam and you saw them darting about in the gloom of that great cobbled area like giant moths.

I remember passing along over there and stopping to gaze in at what appeared as a supernatural spectacle, a kind of Hades without the terror.

All this intense productive activity went into an industry which, having supported a proud independent community for centuries expanded with the introduction of engines, grew and prospered for a short space and then sadly declined. No young men came on to take their fathers' places. Luggers left the harbour. Our own had to go. It was a sad day.

In my young days Mevagissey had a lifeboat, the *James Chisholm*. The lifeboat house – now an aquarium – was opened up every now and then for a practice, and the men were paid five shillings a time for such a rehearsal.

This was a big sum, and a godsend in bad times. The crew would be assembled from whoever was near at hand and ready. Willie Sears Dyer, Father's first cousin was at one time second coxswain, and although lame, moved along the edge of the quay as swiftly as a greyhound. In early times, when hunger was the spectre, he used to rush and collect Father in order that Richard would have five shillings to take home to Mary Sarah.

I can recall the ominous sound of the rocket triumphing over the mighty roar of wind and waves. Father went off once with one boot untied, a bare foot, and braces dangling. He moved swiftly like his cousin, for they were light people.

A real wreck, how painfully exciting it was. The elements had us all in their grip. Swift action ate up fear in the men, ready for the challenge. It wasn't so good for the women, watching and waiting, but hazards of such dimension bred stoicism, and removed the actors from petty concerns for short periods. There was the splendid relief of the return, and the great joy of rescue. What drama!

The village grew, piecemeal and unplanned, its functional pattern and cohesion destroyed by tasteless often ugly dwellings.

Tourism now supersedes fishing, pleasure boats clutter up the harbour and dignity is an outmoded word.

Holiday makers who come in response to glossy brochures, (we are not a congenitally glossy race) are many of them totally unaware of the history buried beneath their innocently ignorant tread. If sometimes we have a feeling that they are trespassing on sacred ground, we must be forgiven.

This closely knit democratic community was overall a conforming one. Men rarely left their wives and children, and the younger ones automatically took on responsibility for the elderly. Almost everyone worked hard. Stealing and violence were rare, and vagrancy practically unknown. Drunkenness, the worst of the vices was confined to the relatively few, and poverty put a firm brake on that anyhow.

People got married for better or worse until death parted them, and many were happy even under the stresses of insecurity. You saw resignation on the faces of those who weren't and they loved their children even if partners were unsatisfactory. Men could escape on to the sea, off for long hours at a time, and in winter for weeks together. Like miners, fishermen have always had their good pals, and faced dangers together in a spirit of comradeship.

There was the usual sprinkling of illegitimates among the population sometimes marked with the unmistakable stamp of their begetters, and you also saw the odd one in families with tell-tale features different from those of his brothers and sisters. 'You know who he is, don't you?' A few illegitimates I always thought to be a healthy addition to the community bringing out the kind of tolerance which might otherwise have lain dormant.

You got some matriarchs among the women. There was one renowned for her domineering who lorded it over a good patient husband. He pushed her round in a wheelchair and died before she did. Once, coming down the steepest part of Polkirt, hanging on for all he was worth, he was greeted by a pal with 'Why doan 'ee let un go, cap'n?'

Many remained single, a state much commoner than now. In big families there would often be a brother and sister left unmarried. Choice was limited, economics perhaps deterred when other circumstance was favourable, and inbreeding probably produced powerful inhibitions. One engagement lasted a lifetime. I can't remember that Harry and Emily ever did get married. After what were often very long courtships, weddings were solemnised, a word I remember spelling out, and deciding I didn't much care for. No one ever had a cousin in the ministry who could help officiate: it was a one-minister ceremony.

Sometimes what seemed to be the most ill-assorted of couples appeared arm-in-arm; so unpredictable are the promptings of love. Gradually however they grew to look and talk like each other. They used to say there was always an old shoe for an old stocking. I wonder.

Crowds appeared chiefly to see the finery, and also to take note of absentees, for Royal groups aren't the only ones to be scrutinised for omissions. (They're at loggerheads, trouble over the will.) The number of bridesmaids varied not so much according to purse as family style, extravagant, simple, unpretentious or flamboyant.

Photographs weren't the craze that they are today, and quiet or gaudy tastes couldn't be reflected in colour. As a family we weren't addicted to photographs, and I cannot have recourse to wedding groups to help me recapture the scenes.

We had no hotels in Mevagissey, and receptions took place in domestic settings. There would be home-cured ham and tongue, and jellies and trifles with extra cream. No strong drinks as far as I remember, cider perhaps. No banquet was unaccompanied by tea, hot and strong. Coffee was not on.

Marj tells me she was impatient for the crowds to be gone after our own wedding receptions, so as to have a good feed of the left-overs. I completely lost my appetite on special occasions.

The one Mevagissey vagrant I remember was a tall completely inoffensive man from a good family. The struggle had been too much for him. I can see him now standing in our garden path outside the kitchen door, his body swathed in ragged coverings, and a piece of stout string round his middle. He wore a disintegrating greasy trilby, and his feet were bound in hessian. I think Mother's distaste was compounded of fear of something she couldn't understand, and a strong revulsion from dirt. Father would remind her that probably Ned would be calling, and would she be sure and give him a 'bit of something'. She lifted her eyes to the ceiling and groaned, but she never sent Ned away empty.

Funerals were very important: the life of the village came to a standstill, and fishermen stayed in from sea to attend. Bearers of the body were chosen from among friends of the dead. If the family could afford it, black gloves were sent to the homes of each bearer, and black edged stationery purchased whereon to thank all those who had helped, or travelled to be present at the funeral. The family dressed in black and friends wore black arm bands and ties.

The day after Father died, I came downstairs in a sort of

daze, to hear Edith and Marion discussing with Mother the question of black clothes which in the thirties were still worn. Should they go to St Austell to get new? I gave vent to one of my intolerant outbursts. 'How in the world can you be thinking of clothes, black, white or any other colour when Father is upstairs lying *dead*?' They reproved me, but to my relief Mother came out with one of her splendid bits of the unexpected. Putting her arm round my shoulder she said, 'Leave her alone. After all, she's right, what does it matter?' Once before, from looking at the sky while rubbing up the pastry, she had turned to me and said, 'Mary, what a strange thing it is that we're here on this earth, isn't it?' I never forgot that moment of wonder that we shared.

It was I suppose, and still is, a strange mixture of real caring, of sacrifice and effort, of powerful superstition and strict adherence to a code of conduct that surrounds death and all its trappings. The mind is baulked by the fact itself, and battles with it unsuccessfully. They are fortunate who can take refuge in the conventions and for whom superstition acts as a buffer against bewilderment, grief, regret. Some of us must struggle on without such distractions.

In most families there appeared those individuals in whom the blood tie operated powerfully to make them faithful visitors of the sick and supporters of the bereaved. It was as if some force drove them to repair the breaches left by loss, to knit together the damaged fabric making it proof against further decay. Henry Dyer, recently dead, son of John Lakeman Dyer, was such a one in our family. He provided help with his car, his time, his advice and a calm presence which was not intrusive. Hartley and Ambrose Pollard, both with strong personalities possess the same keen sense of kinship and achieve a fine faithfulness. 'We are here,' they seem to say. 'We shall not forget.'

Our cousin Mary Blamey was the authority on order of precedence behind the body. Nobody must step out of line. She was outraged to come in and find Marj who had nursed Father, doing the job of laying him out. There were women who held themselves in readiness for this task and daughters should stand back.

In the early days the company would begin singing as the body was borne from the house and then the coffin carried to the dead man's own chapel for a service. I have heard moving tributes on such occasions: men are artists unawares when genuine grief finds adequate expression. Dick Ball had this gift and with a touch of genius brought new life to the dead.

The service over, the body was carried all through the streets to the cemetery, one group of bearers relieving another and then up the almost perpendicular ascent to the grave. Granfer Pollard, who had protested so loudly about the unsuitability of that field, is buried in the steepest part.

I can remember Nell Barron's funeral and the fascination of watching the procession as it left the little doll's house of a dwelling at the bottom of Tregoney Court, very near our own house. They sang 'Shall we gather at the river, the beautiful, the beautiful, the river?' It was an unearthly sound. We were in the land of Beulah, and Nell was about to embark from the 'bourne of time and place' he had shared with us.

It was heavy work all that carrying, and a blessing when it ended, for it must have hastened many a death. All the same a glass hearse is a monstrously awful vehicle, so pretentious, so lonely, and flowers have no place in something so ghastly. A simpler carriage should be devised.

At Father's funeral in the thirties, it was a very comforting thing to hear the tread of his friends before and behind us. One had the feeling of being borne along by the winding procession as it slowly progressed up Church Street, a small army, chiefly of fishermen, all in their navy suits and black ties. 'They moved along the village street with measured step, and slow. They laid him in the cold grey earth. There was no more to do.'

It was a matter of prestige to put on a good meal after a funeral. I always thought hearty appetites to be strangely incongruous at such times, but it seems that if you're living you eat, and especially well after you've buried someone. Every day we go on after the world should have come to an end in sheer horror, built as we seem to be to survive anything and everything, locked up after all in a separate self.

Within the colourful patchwork of our democracy, were

various sub-divisions corresponding chiefly to the different religious denominations, Congregationalists, otherwise Independents, and the three brands of Methodists. These groups provided areas of experience, each with a peculiar character, occasioned not so much by difference of doctrine as by powerful personalities who set their individual stamp upon the 'society'. Perhaps the Congregationalists were rather more intellectual, some of them very solid, substantial citizens. They had a permanent resident minister, and the chapel an exclusive air about it.

Tommy Furse used to play the organ there (it had a far-away sound) and I have heard of someone, who, when blowing for him, became tired of doing the work without ever having any choice of hymn. There came a day when he rebelled: 'You can play what you like,' he said, 'but I'm blowing for "Lead, Kindly Light".'

The Wesleyan Chapel was the largest, and a splendid building housing a thriving society, the pulpit often visited by notorieties, superintendent ministers and the like. One was aware of being an important indeed necessary cell in a large and celebrated body.

The Bible Christians and Reforming Methodists, housed in smaller buildings, along with the Wesleyans, behaved like members of a family, acutely aware of each other's weaknesses. Rivalries flourished, and a certain tension always existed which made the relationship interesting.

We sometimes joined up for a combined service when a great preacher got as far as Mevagissey, treading in the steps of John Wesley, who is known to have visited the village at least seven times. Poor man, he didn't have too good a reception either!

Normally we each went our own ways, for the conforming population was sufficiently large to fill all three buildings. As a Wesleyan child, I regarded Bible Christians to be as foreign, in the religious sense, as Buddhists or Moslems.

As for the Church of England it was utterly remote, something on the periphery of our minds, and physically distant as well, for the church stands well out of the village. The ancient name of Mevagissey was Lanvorrick which means 'a church in the way to the creek'. The Reverend Pollock, the incumbent in my time, officiated once on the *Ibis* when Father consented to bury a friend of Marion's at sea. The weather was poor, and Eddie had to support the good little man, very sea-sick, during the service.

The membership of the church must have included the few better-off citizens, the Conservatives no doubt, and some of the poorer ones, authority and patronage being the joint prerogatives of the Establishment.

Outside all these groups was a pagan fringe, christened, married and buried I suspect by the Church of England, where latitude allows the picking up of all and sundry indiscriminately.

During the week this fringe wasn't so discernible, for working garb reduced saints and sinners to the same species, whereas the spotlight of Sunday searched them out, undisguised.

We have concluded since we grew up that the pagans contained some of the most interesting characters our village produced, amusing, abandoned, surviving without pretence, and of course necessary to give balance to a believing community. Nature loves nothing if not variety. With commendable toughness they had managed to elude the grip of the Wesleys, no mean feat, and a measure of their strong biological resistance.

At the heart of all this were the families, each one distinct, marked by particular gaits, noses, eyes, voices, and traits of character. They were all connected, closely or not so closely, since inbreeding had obtained for centuries. My own paternal grandparents were cousins, and even though our name is a rare one, it seems that the family produced more women, and so the name got lost while the genes survived.

There could never have been much conventional entertaining done in Mevagissey. When Ann Treneer, author of *School House in the Wind*, came in from Gorran she was aware of the watchful eyes of women in doorways. Doors, many of them very close together often stood open, the sun falling on well-scrubbed blue stone or granite steps, and into shining interiors. Familiar figures stood in white aprons or cross-over pinnies, always 'nice and clean'.

Doors were able to stand open even in winter on the south-facing side, for blessed Cornish sunshine tried hard to compensate for the harshness of the winds.

Passing up and down the Cliffside or the street you exchanged greeting with this one and that. My mother never had time to stand in the doorway, and although she didn't leave the village for well over twenty years never visited except at her father's house and her sister's after Granfer died. 'I prefer to sit by my own fire; no "housing" for me.' I fear I too have inherited something which makes me ill-at-ease at morning coffees and afternoon teas.

For the most part people met out-of-doors on the quays, in the streets and at chapel. Of course no-one ever turned you away and children freely entered each other's houses. In winter it was 'Pull fore yer chair; shut 'ome the door.'

We used to be sent with parcels of fish to a few places and particularly to Miss Lelean's up round the corner. (Her father Cap'n Math was related to Mother.) 'My dear, now come in, come in, how are Father and Mother? Thank you. Thank you.'

We also took fish to Cap'n and Mrs at Pen-Pol, and it was placed on the great blue stone of the pantry as big as many a kitchen. I always liked going, so as to have a peep through the open door at the expanse of Turkey carpet, and then to gaze at the china-laden dresser, a shrine at which I worshipped.

Elections strongly gripped the whole community, including many of the women. The pacing up and down the jetty became visibly purposeful, less relaxed, and debate intensified. Father's ardent spirit glowed, for he had a vision of men organising themselves and their work so that freedom and justice could go hand-in-hand the world over.

Indoors the newspaper obtruded on to the table more frequently than was convenient for Mother. 'What! Again!' 'Just one moment, we'll hear what Isaac Foot has to say.' We pinned on rosettes, and once I had made acquaintance with the Tolpuddle Martyrs, it was with a firm touch that I fastened the pin. (I was always one for heroes.)

The Town Hall filled up and overflowed. Some clergyman once said about Mevagissey audiences that they listened so well, they just demanded oratory. Mathy Mills, the Liberal agent, all eyes and eyebrows sped through the streets; he had a small lean figure imbued with resolution.

In early time before Liberalism had been supplanted by Socialism in the real Radicals, Mathy appeared at our door, in conciliatory mood, to speak to Mother, who though it was late, hadn't registered her vote. Father had kept quiet, fearful lest Mother in her ignorance and caprice should go over and cancel out his *Liberal* vote with a Conservative one. He felt some scruples, but couldn't help himself. To his consternation, ill-concealed, she put on her hat and waltzed out of the door. Marj says she knew exactly what Mother was going to do. It came out later she had voted Socialist, one of the few Cornish Labour votes registered I should think, a lost deposit offering. Could that cross have been analysed it must have revealed a strange mixture of mischief, insight, bravado and feminism. The politicians provoke more complex reactions than they realise and it was Father's fault after all that Mother had become educated.

On the same evening Marj was sitting at the kitchen table writing verses on the Election. She produced eight, but we can remember only the last,

And now 'tis after eight
And I must say goodnight
Mathy has just been here
To say 'twas a three-cornered fight.

When I came to study the life of the ancient Greeks I placed a little colony of Athenians on our quays, and allocated a house to Socrates near Pawlyn's Stores where Powell's Emporium now stands, and which is frequented all day long by crowds of visitors licking Kelly's Ices.

When the great thinker gathered his disciples around him it was on our jetty that I placed him and them. The analogy isn't so very far fetched, for Cornish sunshine can have a Mediterranean warmth, and its waters an Aegean blueness, while Mevagissey elders harboured wisdom and a spirit of enquiry behind their far-seeing eyes. Leaning over the cliff wall, with County School history fresh in my mind, I have watched them, four or five abreast pacing slowly up and down on the jetty, in perfect step, turning in the same direction simultaneously, and then all stopping at once inclining towards the one who was propounding something or other. The jetty was their deck.

My father used to walk with John Farran the grocer (high-class) and their talk was chiefly political, John opposing his Conservative creed to Father's Radicalism. They were good friends and enjoyed each other's reasoning, coming together on the ground or public spirit, though nothing on earth would have moved either of them from his own particular stance.

Father walked with Billie Blamey too, the harbour master and at one time coxswain of the lifeboat, large and long legged, his peaked cap well back on his head. Billie was a devil-may-care man of the world with a strong streak of gentleness which made him protective of his friends. I once found a snap of him and Father on the jetty together.

Artists have sculptured a group of figures, which they call Mevagissey Parliament. These figures are of fishermen sitting on the bench at the base of the path above which the very old wooden house projects and which is known as 'under the oss.'

I heard once of a Sunday afternoon session with Johnny Dunn, Dinny Maher, John William Hunkin, Jim Henry Dunn, Harold Barber and Sam Longmaid, who are all long since departed.

It was late October and getting chilly. Sundays can become melancholy as the sun sets. They had spoken of the Sunday joints at the bakehouse, and how far they reflected current economics, discussed election candidates and their chances, picked to pieces the new houses erected on the north side, and then ten minutes passed in silence. Sunday afternoon was long. 'What's the time?' from a watchless member. Dinnie consulted a silver heirloom and pronounced it as being ten to four. Johnny unslung his gold chain and made the time twenty to. There followed something approaching a dispute; Dinnie was having no reflection cast on his silver timepiece, and proposed having a look at the Post Office clock. He strolled off, but ah! he didn't come back.

'Now,' said Johnny, 'I am a man of a few words, but I know my watch was right, and for why? I had set it by the Post Office.' Pause. 'And sometheen rose within me,' he continued, 'which said "I will not be done, and I stick to it". A Watch chain,' he continued 'what is it? A piece of string would do as well, but there 'tis, we wear chains.'

'I believe you're vain, Johnny,' and Jim Henry screwed up his wry face. He wore his habitual cap and jersey, being one of those with no particular respect for the Sabbath.

'No, no,' said Johnny, 'today is Sunday and we do put on our bit o' best and our chain.'

That evening Johnny stood in his Methodist pew singing 'Blessed assurance, Jesus is mine. Oh what a foretaste of glory divine.' He had beautiful skin had Johnny, being of a placid disposition, and he trusted his Lord as he did the Post Office clock. No false prophets could ever shake that faith.

II

Home, Family, Friends

At the bottom of Tregoney Hill you will find a shop with deep-seated windows where silver jewellery made on the premises, is displayed on velvet pads. That shop is the ground-floor of the cottage in which I was born, the seventh child, and where I lived for the first six years of my life.

You stepped down two wide stone steps from the street into the living room flanked on the right by a small work-place we called the play-room and where mother did her washing. In the far left-hand corner of the living room was a Cornish range, and an open staircase ran up horizontally at the back of the house to two more storeys. Each one contained two very low rooms identical with those on the ground floor, the smaller one being reached through the larger. The bigger one on the first floor was the parlour and had an Adam fireplace.

It was all very cosy and shining. The fire was always in, and the bellows in frequent use. Father would take me on his left knee, and steady the bellows on his right. The blowing provided a comforting motion, the rhythms of which he adapted to those of whatever verse he chose to chant.

I remember, I remember
The house where I was born
The little window where the sun
Came peeping in at morn.

Baa Baa Black Sheep
Have you any wool?
Yes Sir Yes Sir
Three bags full.

His arm was strong, his voice low, the fire red, and the moments full of magic. The table had a green plush cloth with a fringe and bobbles. It was laid when evening fell, and a brass oil-lamp placed in the centre.

In that last hour before bed-time, Dick would take out the big slate and lead pencil which were our only writing materials, and entertain me with drawings of gulls and starlings, dogs and cats, cows and pigs, sometimes putting names to them which I repeated. What excitement as the eye appeared on the head, or the tail curled on the body. Expensive toys could never elicit more enthusiasm or delight. There was no appeasing my appetite for more. 'Write another one, please, please.' Never did an elder brother show more patience with a little sister than Dick did with me.

Arch and Eddie would sit carving small wooden punts and luggers with their pen-knives, paring away with great concentration, totally absorbed, while Mother sometimes helped with neat strong sails for the finished articles. Usually though she was darning, darning, darning.

Father stood with his back to the fire, and enjoyed giving his older girls lessons in spelling. 'Break up your words into syllables,' he would say, 'and see each one separate. Then pronounce your way through.'

My earliest memory of entering into the life of the community was at the outbreak of war in 1914. I was three. A great solemn crowd in a dense mass had congregated on the Town Bridge surrounding the pump, standing on it, and filling every cranny and doorway of the surrounding buildings. In the centre was a small group of boys about to march off to battle. The local band struck up. They began to move. I stood outside Tilly Warren's shop, holding my mother's hand, distressed by the tears which coursed down her thin anxious face.

These boys were sons of a closely-knit classless society where ties of blood, of interdependence, of shared fear of death and joy-in-life were as strong as any human connections could ever be. Spectres of starvation and drowning, delight in green country, bright flowers, ripe fruits, hot sunshine, fair breezes and great love for each other had made of these people one body, threatened now by calamitous wounding of war. Dollie tells me that she and her friends, then in their tenth year, were amongst those who went to the top of Second Hill to see the last of the boys.

I remember the outlines of my mother's lithe figure as she drew the blind that evening, and the atmosphere of the room where intense thought was concentrated on those shut out from home perhaps for ever. A poem of Edward Thomas's has taken me back to that room many times throughout my adult life. It is 'The Owl' and the last verse runs

And salted was my food and my repose
Salted and sobered too by the bird's voice
Speaking for all who lay under the stars
Soldiers and poor, unable to rejoice.

I was about five when Edith went to Cardiff to stay with Auntie Etta in Whitchurch Road. She came back with a doll purchased in one of the city's great stores. It was of china, had rosy cheeks, and wore an apple-green crêpe dress. I played with it on the evening of her return, sitting in the sun on the blue stone door-step. Suddenly a great chasm appeared in the round head: in an agony of incredulity I gazed into the hole. Edith had gone out. I took the casualty to Mother and wept.

'It isn't the doll, Mother,' I said, 'it's Edith; she will be so hurt.'

I went to bed, and lay awake, consumed with remorse. I hadn't really wanted that doll. I wasn't much for dolls, and I had to convince myself that I hadn't been careless. Mother explained when Edith came in, and I heard my sister's step on the stairs.

In a moment her arms were around me, and we both cried. 'There, there, my handsome,' she said, 'who cares? It's only an old doll. Go to sleep now and don't fret.'

Another time I made use of Edith to tell Mother when, having been bathed and dressed in clean underwear and a white voile dress, I sat in a bowl of tar. My knickers clung to my thighs, and the tar dripped down my legs. I heard Edith and Mother laughing inside the kitchen door as my predicament was being described.

In 1916 when Dick was fifteen, he fell ill with pneumonia, and his bed brought down into the parlour and a fire lit in the Adam fireplace. Dr Grier came and stayed a long time. Sheets were hung round the bed as a screen, and when everything else had failed, Doctor suggested that they have recourse to poultices. A poultice was made as follows: A piece of linen was spread on a board. Boiling water was then poured into an already heated bowl, and linseed meal added to the water, a little at a time, and stirred with a spatula. The consistency was right if the bowl was left clean on removal of the poultice. It was turned out on to the linen ¼ inch in thickness, a margin of one inch being left all round. This was turned down over the poultice, the spatula dipped in boiling water, smeared over the surface and the whole rolled and carried to the bedside between hot plates. The poultice was applied to the affected part of the chest, covered with jaconet, or brown paper, then a woollen cover, and supported finally by a many-tailed bandage made of flanelette strips. Poultices were very comforting, and a most effective method of treatment. There were no drugs in those days and life-saving was an arduous business involving hours of close watching and waiting.

Downstairs the family sat round the table their faces, wet with tears, laid on the plush cloth. A great silence prevailed. I remember moving from one to another, touching each lightly on the shoulder, anxious, awestricken. Something terrible was happening beyond their power to communicate. I got no answer, but somebody held my hand. The crisis came. Our Dick survived, and reappeared as a little white stick, smiling feebly. Howard Dunn arrived with black grapes. This rare expensive fruit was supposed in those days to make blood. I imagine it as a kind of secular version of transubstantiation, the sort of miracle, which, along with all other Popish superstitions, I firmly rejected when theology cropped up as a branch of history at the County School.

Dr Grier was an excellent physician and a great friend of Mevagissey mothers and their families. Three years before Dick's illness when Marjorie was born, he saved Mother's life, and her gratitude took the form of reverence for him. She was in bed for a whole month, and assiduously that good man attended her.

Nurse Furse was there too in her faded green uniform. Tall and angular, she was of foreign extraction and by that I mean English, not Cornish. She had flat feet, a flat face and a flat voice. Excellently unsentimental, faithful and sensible, she was endowed with a Rock of Ages quality hewn for service to a needy community. Her pronouncements were without camouflage. 'You'll never rare her, Mrs Lakeman,' she said, when she delivered Marj, the last of us. Mother was forty-four and she hadn't wanted this her eighth child, but she clung to the little life with great tenacity and tenderness. Those two were very close throughout the years and always sat next to each other at table, Marjorie waiting to see what Mother chose to eat and taking just that for herself. When Mother peppered her egg (always lavishly) Marj peppered hers. 'Ah,' Mother would say, 'If I were to drink jollop (jallop) that cheeld would do the same.'

Nurse Furse was still alive at Kopje Top when Marjorie took up nursing. Before leaving home she went to see Nurse Furse to tell her what she was doing, and along with a blessing, received two nursing books as a parting gift.

As for Dr Grier he was more than a physician. He went in for architecture and the little white Mediterranean-looking houses at Ava are of his design. They are more attractive and decorative than solid or functional, but the trees and shrubs which he planted in the drive have grown and blossomed handsomely, justifying his faith that the Cornish soil and climate would respond to his artistic aspirations. He loved Mevagissey, and became as good as a native.

In his early years he had been anything but a puritan, and perhaps it was because of this that he became so religious in his old age. I met him once outside the post office wearing a smart plaid tweed cloak (he had excellent taste) and he asked me if I was saved. It was a question I think he put to most people. My answer was, 'Yes doctor, of course!' He smiled with great warmth, relieved and delighted that one more of his 'infants' would be gathered home. I was right to conceal from him the fact that I was already an unbeliever.

The bay at Mevagissey. *A sketch by Peter Markey*

The Outer Harbour

Mevagissey Board School. *A sketch by Peter Markey*

Empire Day 1922.

It was in 1912 that Marion went to work in the post office. As soon as I could walk I used to travel down the street, turn right at the corner, make for the shop door, and peering in, call for my sister.

The girls indulged me, and if Mrs Roberts wasn't there I'd be lifted on to the counter and invited to talk. The proprietress would however soon appear, and with a deprecatory H'm H'm H'm, discourage further interruption of the unpaid work her band of employees was expected never to stop doing. Miss Ada Lelean, senior assistant and Mother's cousin, smilingly benevolent would have permitted more of such distractions. I had to wait until evening for Edith to come home because by this time she was at school in St Austell.

Marion's Thursday afternoons, her only time-off, were spent entirely in cleaning the house and generally helping Mother. I can remember the chambers all being brought down and washed in hot soapy water. By evening there would perhaps be a fresh bunch of primroses tastefully arranged in a basin, or a few beech leaves in an old-fashioned jug standing in the window-seat. What slog it all was to be sure, but enthusiasm for life, and the hope of better times were never extinguished completely in anxiety or anguish, although of these there was plenty. All the world was in travail just then as it is now, bitter travail indeed.

Marion was to leave for Truro Post Office when I was about six, and soon after that, Father's only brother Will died. Uncle Will had worked on the boats that brought back the wounded from France, a gruelling task which broke his tender heart.

One of the accessories of funerals in those days was black-edged envelopes. Mother supplied me with those left over from Uncle Will's and I used them for letters to absent relatives. The mourning went on for quite a long time until envelopes ran out and Mevagissey news took serial form.

A few yards from our door was the fish factory, the managing director being Mr Cregoe, who lived at Portmellon. Mr Cregoe represented *Big Business*; Industry Proper, Rulers, Strangers, Employers, another class of mortals who had something to do with the rich man in his castle, and the poor man at his gate. Remember that the Mevagissey fishermen were always their own bosses.

It was a small inoffensive factory, which emitted pungent pure smells of cured pilchards. The air became heavy with tasty molecules, giving off that exciting odour associated with Scottish visitors who came to teach the Mevagissey women how to do the job. They were tall and graceful, wore long skirts and clogs, and congregated in small groups with a reserve equal to our own. Coming down Board School Hill we were met by that pilchardy smell, borne on the winds, filling our nostrils, reminding us that life and work were proceeding, and that food was at the centre of both.

We used to go inside the great factory doors to play. It was spacious, warm, clean and safe and nobody turned us out. We called Mr Cregoe's carriage the chariot, associating it with Elijah, and when it arrived or departed, our activities were suspended for a session of staring. There'd be Mr Cregoe, regal on the box, and behind Mrs Cregoe in bonnet and cape, and their Mongoloid daughter, small and fascinating, carrying great age and immaturity in her yellow face. Dick decided that Mr Cregoe was God, only without a beautiful countenance, and Mother suggested that his swallow-tail coat did something to take off the plainness. I suppose she meant it deflected attention therefrom.

Mr Cregoe retired and left Portmellon, and sold his chariot to Mr Willie Prynn, the local coal merchant and Sunday School Superintendent, but somehow Mr Prynn couldn't carry on the tradition with any degree of comfort to himself, or conviction for us. The chariot looked less imposing: the faces of the new owners weren't plain enough, and there were no velvets, laces, or feathers. The occupants had a slightly embarrassed air, and we suspected that sacred ground had been invaded.

What is more, chariots were just about to be overtaken by cars, so that time and change were in league to render Mr Prynn's enterprise out-of-date, its inappropriateness endorsed by the revolution in locomotion just round the corner. What happened to the chariot we never knew: we see it still rolling out of the factory gate, manned by the Cregoes in all their glory, representative of an age, of a class, of a life that is gone.

In our playroom, or, more accurately washhouse, was another vehicle, our own chariot which we called a dray. It was a large fish-box reinforced underneath, and to which were attached four pram-wheels and a strong rope handle. The interior was padded with an old blanket. It was taken well up the hill beyond Ernie Crowle's barber's shop; I was securely tucked inside and the dray went rocketing down the slope with Dick and Arch, arms outstretched, holding on to the handle.

At the bottom of the street and across the main road was May Ball's shop inside the open door of which stood a collection of galvanised pails and baths. One day the dray was given a mighty push and steered straight over the step into the hardware. I remember my bewilderment amongst the deafening din, and can see May's face as she bent over me. Having assured herself I was unhurt, she rushed out of the door shouting, 'You spurticles [mischievous boys] you spurticles! Mrs Lakeman, where be to? They'll kill that cheeld.'

Until then it had only been the odd iron hoop that had intruded amongst its kind. The rattle at those times was something terrible, and the hoop seemed almost to be a real playmate waiting to be rescued. I can see it now fallen on its side against the great wooden counter, the innocent instrument of boyish pranks, demanding release from its undeserved captivity, longing to be on the move again.

It was impossible for those boys not to tease May when her cries were so agonising, her gestures so dramatic. (She had poor sight and wore dark glasses.) The dividends of entertainment derived from provoking her were exceptionally high, and my brothers could not resist such rewards, nor the ruse of using me to break the tide of her wrath. She had a tender heart under a severe exterior, and they knew it.

The following incident I don't remember, but Dollie tells me that the playroom once housed a great box mattress about eight inches deep which Father bought at a sale in Portmellon, and got home by some means or other. It was a fine purchase, but a bigger nuisance, filling the playroom, too big to go up the stairs or to fit any bed, in fact the whitest of white elephants. Father's judgement was usually so good, it was an unknown thing for him to do anything silly, but he had shown himself to be fallible, and had fallen from grace.

To Mother's delight Dick stood by the mattress, inspected it, tapped it, praised it and then in ringing tones began to auction it, Mother laughed until she cried. It was the first time Father had ever been successfully challenged, and Dick cleverly wrapped up the criticism in a great package of wit. 'A shilling, I'm bid. Any advance on a shilling? A fine mattress. Well sprung. Big enough I'd say. Come from a good home. Only two shillings! What's the world coming to?' The mattress was stored somewhere, and reappeared later when we moved to 17 Tregoney Hill where it did excellent service for many years under the title of 'The Plains of Ono.' So in a way Father was justified after all.

Edith's bicycle was also housed in the playroom. In 1909 she had won a scholarship to St Austell County School, and I can dimly remember her going off to Gramma's to do her homework. Times were very bad then, it was a hand-to-mouth existence for our family, and for the village in general. Edith couldn't play any games at school; there wasn't enough money for such luxuries as hockey-sticks. She went off in the mornings, poor child, on bread and sugar. She had to excuse herself to the headmistress, and told a story about having a weak heart. The irony of it was that her heart was the strongest part of her, literally and metaphorically.

When she won her scholarship Father confided in Mother that he'd willingly sell his bed to be able to send her to school. 'Oh no you don't,' Mother said, 'it happens to be half mine, and I shall keep it.' She often had to correct him when his splendid aspirations ran away with him.

Amidst severe material deprivation, Edith was loved and encouraged and watched over by her parents and dear Gramma Lakeman, and adored by us younger ones. She would gather us round her, and invite us, wide-eyed and worshipful, to accompany her into a rosy future, when we'd all live together in a beautiful house with spacious rooms, having big windows with lace curtains. Fires would always be burning and in a large kitchen we'd have a tall dresser filled with the best china. There'd be no more sharing of bedrooms, and wardrobes with full-length mirrors would contain clothes not passed on from anyone else. Besides which, we'd have a large chest-of-drawers each.

Strange to say her imagination faltered when it came to floor-coverings. They would be of the best quality linoleum with bright home-made rugs laid thereon. Neither was there any mention of servants. We'd all take our share of the work, a part of her dream which has been most accurately fulfilled maintaining the proletarian ethic intact.

Our fantasies had great values for survival no doubt, and I imagine we enjoyed our dreams far more than the wealthy can ever have delighted in actualities.

To the right of us at Tregoney Hill lived Mrs Burt, mother of a large family of boys, and Ida. With them were Granfer and Granny Lean. Granfer Lean was the caretaker of our chapel for many years. I can just remember him filling the paraffin lamps at the ends of the pews.

It was a tall house, theirs, dwarfing our own and tiled to the ground in grey slate. A big cobbled area led to the Mill opening, where the smooth oval stones shone after the rain. At the heart of Mrs Burt was that particular brand of goodness, compounded of humility and insight, which marks the few saints to appear among mortals. Her comprehending eyes looked out from a worn face framed in soft wispy hair. I never saw her in a hat or coat. She wore slippers and a faded wrap-over apron, and seemed never to go beyond the Town Bridge. George her husband was a jouter (a hawker of fish) and gone at daybreak in his cart. Malya (Amelia) his mother, lived two doors away, wore a black waist apron, and carried a huge basket of fish as big as herself.

George, a tall, heavy, very shy man liked his pint. Father, half his size and addicted only to tea, was a friend as well as a neighbour: Mrs Burt was able to confide in him and he understood. I believe it was for his sake that she loved us all. I used to go in after breakfast and sit with her by the fire while she washed and dressed Melville. The sun poured in the big window and we'd drink sugary tea. I became her little girl. Her pace was slower than that of my mother, whose drive was perpetually at war with every speck of dirt or disorder. The policeman once said that on his nightly beat he noticed Mrs Lakeman's light was always the last to go out. With Mrs Burt time took on the quality of eternity: so many and acute were her anxieties, so precarious her life, that she survived only by looking above and beyond. There was little or no religion of the orthodox brand in that household, but a philosophy of uncomplaining love and resignation prevailed. We noticed that the Sabbath next door was like an ordinary day and that Mrs Burt would sit in her window knitting on Sunday afternoons. She had nothing of censure to fear from her immediate neighbours, and must have known that flexibility underlay their conforming exterior.

Mrs Meek lived across the cobbled space and deserved her name more by reason of being born a Dunn than through any married meekness. She had black velvety eyes and was the very essence of neatness and propriety, tidied by early afternoon and owning a front door that I believe was varnished. She fancied genteel speech, and once said she had done to her 'huttamost'. Ever afterwards, all of us, and Mother in particular, did just that instead of our best.

History has swallowed up much of that dense bit of street, altering the contours of buildings, dispelling some of the darkness of interiors, and claiming not only the last generation for oblivion, but a good percentage of our own. A restaurant, a house agent's and a jeweller's have stepped in to that humble domain, and demolition has been the necessary fate of the buildings by the factory entrance where Jim and Mrs Bullen lived.

Marjorie was always a good mixer and had many pals who entered our house and took her into theirs. She used to go with May (Bullen) up the stone steps and down a long rickety corridor to stand at an open door and look in on Mrs Bullen who was then very ill. We realise now that she must have been suffering from dropsy, and there were no relieving drugs in those days to disperse the water. Having exchanged smiles with Mrs Bullen from a respectful distance, saddened and awed, Marj went straight in to Mother to tell her about the pale face into which she had gazed. When, twenty-five years later she began health visiting in Taunton it was that very face that came back to her, and she knew she had never ceased to be drawn, by some compelling force, into the presence of the sick and the dying.

Ernie Barron, tall, and a little older than we, lived in these same buildings. The illegitimate son of Bessie, and a spastic, he dominated the scene, all arms and legs and orders. We made his life happy by deferring to him: children have civilising propensities as well as savage impulses and cope with the unfamiliar and deprived with the adaptability characteristic of the young.

Next door on our left lived the Marshalls, but although we were on very good terms we didn't ever enter their house. In fact Mother and Father did no visiting at all except to their parents. My mother worked from early morn to late at night, and for about twenty years or more never went out of the village.

Mr Marshall, Jim, was the dustman, or scavenger as he was called in those days before so many euphemisms had debilitated the language, so that the Marshalls had a regular wage, and were often better off than we, Mrs Marshall had very dark hair screwed back in a bun in her neck as was the fashion then, and her front teeth were very large. She rarely smiled.. Lily Maud, Marj's contemporary, actually had a tricycle which she generously shared with her friend. Not one streak of meanness or possessiveness there. In the very poor you often find an abandon and recklessness equivalent to that manifested by the rich. In one a sense of values has never had a chance to take root; in the other it was not required.

Lily Maud and Marjorie would pedal up and down the empty street and then chase Ernie into the precincts of the factory, he leaping like a tropical insect out of the way of the fast-moving wheels.

There was a little shop opposite us, a grocery store I think, and a flight of steps at the side which led up to the house of Mr and Mrs Martin Dunn, who childless, had adopted Albert Hunt. Martin had brought home his wife from the East Coast, Lowestoft probably, whither the Mevagissey boats had formerly ventured, so there was a foreign rather more strident accent in our midst, and a slightly different way of life in that upper storey, more easy-going, with meals that were less regular. Immigrants were few and kept their separate identities.

Further down was Johnny Whatty's barber's shop, marked by a painted pole, where shaving and haircutting were subsidiary to fraternisation and gossip, the room serving as a kind of club. It was a gloomy place, but warm, having a coal fire, and benches round the walls. When I came to read Dostoievsky, that building dark and mysterious was the one in which I placed Raskolnikoff brooding on the necessity to commit his crime.

I remember Dennis Maher and Sam Williams as the veterans so to speak, Johnny's henchmen: you could always be sure to see one of those two either going in or coming out. The shop stayed open very late. Johnny made no money, but remained the poor proprietor of this classless salon. Harry, one of his sons, who later developed into a very genial popular citizen, used to dance outside in a plaid skirt, and shout 'Tiss me ass! Tiss me ass.'

Over that shop lived the Rickards, brown-eyed and merry, a very big family indeed with royal names among them of Rex and Victoria. They had good looks and good tempers and were light on their feet. Respect for royalty was probably part of their being C of E and not so inimical to authority as we, who with non-conforming principles were more critical of society's architecture.

The Williamses lived there too, Olive and her sisters, very graceful like film stars. Janie Fulfit, my school pal, was the only child of Harry Fulfit and Janie (Furse) who had been crippled by poliomyelitis, and they lived over what is now Lloyd's Bank. Janie, the daughter has told me that her mother was at one time taken under the wing of a clever uncle, who introduced her and brother Sam to poetry and other branches of culture.

Janie Junior was never allowed out to play. I always felt disconsolate when I saw her disappearing up those stairs, lost to me as she was then, until in the morning the school-bell reunited us, throwing us together into the freedom of learning.

Down from the Marshalls and opposite Janie's was the

habitation of Mr and Mrs Eli Cloke, parents of Philip and Will. Mrs Cloke sang with great sweetness and they had a gramophone in their house with a loud-speaker horn, an exotic possession which matched Eli's impeccable manners, dress, and mode of speech. Later on they bought Mrs Alma Robins's house on the Town Bridge which Philip still runs as a restaurant, a refuge in winter for the fishermen who have developed a morning coffee habit, borrowed no doubt from the visitors.

They sit there engaged in topical conversation. My brother Eddie, a gregarious being, relaxes and enjoys a middle-class leisureliness, and even Dick has succumbed to a mid-morning break.

It occurs to me now how very thickly-populated our little street was, twice the number of people in half as many buildings as now. Each dwelling emitted a stream of human beings, old, middle-aged and young, all stamped with a family likeness, variations on a Cornish theme, the products of inbreeding over centuries, selected by evolutionary forces for survival.

In large conurbations outside the county I still feel an alien, and can communicate well only with those whom circumstances has taught to be practical in a sense different from the conventional norm. One lives as it were, on a mental extremity, equivalent to the rocky peninsula which the Romans left to its wild and dreamy devices, with the great seas dashing against its granite obduracy.

I once found a second home in the Hebrides, rocky, dangerously safe, open and free, with small sunny pockets of security where self and surroundings merged in perfect adaptation and ecological harmony. You could leave your doors unlocked, they told us, and when you asked your way, they not only instructed you, but in silent companionship went along with you until the crucial turning was passed.

How all we families at the bottom of Tregoney Hill survived is a mystery which dieticians, pediatricians and psychologists together might possibly unravel. Fish, apples, fresh air and sunshine, loving parents, indulgent grandparents, and conscientious doctors must all have played their part in saving us, and many more from premature death.

As the boys grew older they left the street and were busy on the quays and in the boat. They went off wooding and blackberrying too and always they took me with them. There'd be a group including Willie Husband, Ambrose Pollard (our cousin) and Colin Blamey, and I was carried on one or other of their shoulders, but chiefly Dick's, his hands grasping my ankles.

We often went 'up Valley Park' past Willie Body's fenced garden where straying loganberries thrust through the cracks, flowered, and provided us with a handful of fruits. Then we passed along by Mrs Smitham's small estate, where the gate was always wide open, and entry never forbidden. It was a veritable Garden of Eden. What roses, what odours, what burgeoning of everything beautiful within, and how green was the lawn beneath the massive chestnut tree. Sunshine fell with the density of paint, and never was a sky so blue, nor hedges more flowery. I was given a treacle tin with a handle of strong string and it swung on my wrist.

We passed through a wide gate and emerged on to a green field which belonged to old Mr Williams. It was known as the Piece, but I always thought of it as the Peace. Stored in my head it has provided me with a background for many a rural scene in literature.

Elm trees on the hedges the curls of their trunks intertwining rose high into the sky, the grass was lush, the cows contented, and in the distance the sea sparkled, that other element from which we were never far removed.

I remember Dick once placing me on top of the wide hedge and asking if I would sit there for a while, and not move until they came back. It seemed years that they had been absent. I couldn't even hear their voices, and then at last, oh joy, there they were filling my tin with blackberries so that I could make an offering to Mother myself.

On Monday mornings Dick always stayed home from school to help Mother with the washing, lightening the load with his company as much as by his help. I think he must have half lived her life for her. 'Mother, what can I do before I go?' was his cry. When Arch, Dollie and Eddie came home they would help take the clothes in big flaskets made of withes right up Tregoney Hill and into the Leat Field, built on now, its greenness despoiled. There were the poles and lines, and they pinned up the load, sheets, towels, men's striped drawers, knickers with lace edging, liberty bodices, twill shirts, hand-knitted socks, sea-boot stockings, flannelette night gowns, and much besides. Early they developed the requisite skill.

I must tell you that sheets and tablecloths, everyone's, were made of flour bags stitched together. In time the blue stamp on them faded to nothing, but the dye being strong, the tell-tale lettering disclosed the origins of our linen for longer than it was kind of it to do. What mattered however was that flour-bags were mighty strong, and obliged by becoming soft and white with boiling. The twill shirts it seems were also lined with flour-bags.

Dollie took the starched bits in an enamel bowl and laid them on the grass or bushes. It would all be gathered in before dusk. I remember trailing on behind them, hurrying on my short legs, and then picking up the handkerchiefs, doing my share, happy as long as they were near. The clothes were light now and smelled of the sun, two flaskets full.

Eddie had by this time become a wanderer on quay, beach and cliff. Earlier he had worn an iron on his leg for a suspected TB knee and was much indulged by the fishermen. He used to come home with what Mother called a high-water mark, a rim of dried salt on his boots, and his socks saturated with brine. I suppose the economics of footwear has always harassed working-class mothers. It certainly did ours. She used to slap Eddie's wet socks about his legs, unless he was able to arrest the attack with 'Mother, have you heard that so and so is dead?' Sometimes he would cry, 'Kill me, kill me. That's right. Go on. Do it.' We remained unmoved, knowing very well that Mother's castigation was quite disproportionate to the cleverness of his tactics, that he would come out of these encounters unscathed, and ready for the next affray.

Marion tells me that once, when times were so very bad at the beginning of the war, she had the idea of selling marinated fish. She was at work in the post office and took on the mores of commerce therefrom. Small fat pilchards were split, washed and laid one on top of the other, backbone remaining, in a large earthenware pan, and then cooked slowly for hours in vinegar, spices and bayleaves. Mother was a practised hand. 'We could make a little money, Mother,' Marion said. 'Why not?'

So a notice went on the door. 'Marinated fish sold here.' It sold only too well, but returns were small and the business instinct, never strong, and planted in uncultivated soil, died a natural death. Mother worked far too hard already, and after a while the boys were old enough to man the boat and began to catch fish. We still had our own pan of marinated however, and very delicious it was.

Grandparents had played an important part in the lives of my older brothers and sisters, but I just managed to make the acquaintance of three of them before they died, and can remember their physical appearance, carriage, and voices.

In my time Granfer and Gramma Lakeman lived in the end house of Prospect Place the big red building on School Hill. Gramma was a little lady who wore a black bonnet and cape and carried a small round basket.

She used to hide her pension book under her cape, for she was never really reconciled to receiving anything from the State. Her children and grandchildren regarded her with something like veneration. She was wise, sensitive and scrupulous in all her dealings shedding about her an aura which forbade crooked thinking, careless speech or devious action.

Gramma I imagine took a tragic view of life and found the weight of suffering which the years accumulated too heavy to be balanced by experience of joy, though she did not complain. She was happiest when pottering in her little garden, for she had come from the country, Kestle, where her father Granfer Johns had combined the working of a small holding with carpentry and wood-carving. She used to wear a man's cap when outside attending to her plants. I remember the moss roses, the boy's love and lavender, and the large velvety golden petals of her gilly flowers. Her grandchildren called on her daily and she shared all their joys and sorrows.

Edith went always to Gramma's to do her homework,

receiving there the loving individual attention; and benefiting from the peace that our own establishment could not provide. There were a few books and papers in that little house. Granfer had some works on natural history beautifully illustrated in delicate colours; he preferred this to theology and I'm sure would have made a good disciple of Darwin and Huxley.

There was a splendid copy of *Pilgrim's Progress* like the one which Maggie studied in *The Mill on the Floss*. Along with most others of their generation, they were thoroughly well acquainted with Christian's pilgrimage. Gramma read the *Sunday Companion* and *Methodist Recorder*, but was not a pious woman. Creeds sat lightly on something deeper, and I know that Granfer was never beguiled by dogmas.

Adapting to the community, and over a long period earning the sort of prestige which results from consistently self-effacing, courageous behaviour, allows certain individuals, and Gramma was one, to take a strong habit of mind into regions beyond overt social patterns, and enter into an advanced shaping of the self to the self. The outside world recedes and imperatives come chiefly from within. Gramma walked so to speak a tight-rope of moral exigency, along which she was propelled by fine distinctions of judgement.

The psychologists have it all explained, and I am more than ready to follow them, even to extremes of determinism. Yet it is a relief, at the same time to escape into the revelation of poetry, and enjoy the individual quality of a particular person's mental climate. It is Emily Dickinson who best lights up for me the remotest corners of the mind, and it was of Gramma Lakeman that I thought when first I found this verse.

The soul unto itself   Secure against its own
Is an imperial friend   No treason it can fear
Or the most agonising spy   Itself its sovereign, of itself
Any enemy could send.   The soul should stand in awe.

Unfailingly kind to my hard-working independent mother, Gramma made a deep impression on her daughter-in-law,

who came to love her. Indeed my mother cared much for all
Father's family, and scarcely without knowing it, put up a
protective barrier round them. She knew that life could never
be easy for the kind of people they were.

It was before we left Lower Tregoney Hill that Granfer
Pollard died in the very month and year of the Russian
Revolution 21st October, 1917. His nickname was Lion, and
he owned and occupied the house with the door in the roof
which appears now on so many picture postcards and recently
even on hearth-rugs.

The house had been in his wife's family for hundreds of
years. Mary, the mother of his family died soon after Mother,
her sixth, possibly seventh child was born. He later married
his wife's older sister who brought up the children and whom
he treated well. He was however a lonely man whose heart did
not heal. His intelligence of the pragmatic variety served him
well as a district councillor, and there are still a few left, the
Farrans for instance, who remember his reputation for
fearlessness and straightforward dealings. His passions ran
deep, and he could wait with an iron will and utter disregard
of people's opinions for tides of events to change their course,
and justify his actions.

In his early years he was a great Radical and acquainted
himself with history by means of encyclopaedias over which he
pored for hours on end. His interests were chiefly secular,
though he played his part in the Congregational Church
where his fine tenor voice filled the building with a roar like
the sea itself and especially in 'Eternal light, Eternal light.
How pure the soul must be!' which was his favourite hymn.

A bill was once sent him for a sum of money he had already
paid and he allowed his so-called creditor to bring him to
court. It was there that Granfer produced his perfectly kept
books and a receipt for the money. My own father would
never have humiliated anyone in this fashion. I once asked
him whether the 70 times 7 of the Bible really meant 490 in the
context of forgiveness. He smiled slowly and said, 'I think you
already know my tar, that it means you go on for ever.'

Visitors must surely look with surprise at the precipitous
cemetery which appears on the left-hand side at the bottom of

the hill as you enter Mevagissey. They might perhaps like to go up and try walking down the grass. This burial ground has been full for many a long year and looks beautiful in the sunshine. Our young ones used to call it the Palace.

Granfer Pollard bitterly opposed the purchase of that field, the cheapness of which recommended it to the majority of the councillors. 'In burying your dead,' he said, 'have you no regard for the living? Can't you feel the weight of coffins on the upper slope of that field?'

I saw the strained faces of fishermen ascending that steep path many years later, resting and starting again and felt my Granfer's indignation rise in me. He was always against short-term cheapness. Dick tells me that he helped carry Howard Dunn (a very big man) from the Church along the road and well up that hilly field, and when they got to the grave, regret for Howard and exhaustion from bearing him so far, suggested to him that it might be as well to fall into the pit along with his friend.

Once when a Trustee appeared at our house on chapel business, he said about me to Mother, 'Ah! She's more of a Lion, isn't she?' Mother was highly indignant. 'The impudence of that man,' she said. 'How dare he!'

Granfer died when I was six and an air of finality surrounds my memories of him, sitting with a rug round his knees at No 3 The Cliff. We used to visit every Sunday evening after chapel. There was a powerful indefinable smell that hit you as you opened the heavy door and stepped down the steep stair. It was a compound of age, polish, tar, brine and crab, and the atmosphere verily shimmered. The staircase, two, one on each side, led down to what could be used as two dwellings and in fact throughout the years accommodated older or younger branches of the family. We stepped gingerly down the left-hand side to meet the grandfather clock at the base. It had a brass face with a moon and registered time of a denser nature than the passing moments. Behind its enigmatic face there seemed to be an intense and secret life as of an impartial observer watching, always watching. Granfer watched you too, keenly, scanning your features assessing your potential. Cornish people love their children, and recognise their individuality, eschewing Victorian suppressive modes of treatment.

In the Cornish range the fire burned summer and winter alike, and on the right-hand wall stood a tall dresser with glass doors. The china inside was various, the jugs of odd shapes and with pictures on them. The window looked down on the inner harbour and here Marj and I sat, one on each side quite still, while the weekly conversation between our elders ate up the hour. The quay below served as Mevagissey Promenade where all the world took its airing. There were couples of all ages, family groups, gangs of boys, knots of young ladies, and always the solitary ones passing by the Watch House, and out through the Quay Door to the outer Arm. In they came again, fronts now instead of backs, a familiar stream of perambulating humans, and we the fascinated audience, observing figures, gaits, expressions, and every fashion of every season, slavishly followed or grandly ignored.

Sometimes the floor of the room would open in a two foot square where the trap-hatch, fitted with a brass ring, led by a steep ladder into the cellar below, once a storage place for contraband. Up the hatch went, and the dark-haired head of a cousin having appeared, an arm would rest the hatch against the wall. 'Wha' Cheer.'

It was time to go. Bed-time for us now. Good-night, Father. Good-night, Mary Sarah, Richard. Good-night, Granfer. The same penetrating look. Good-night, my dears.

Tom Pollard would have liked Dylan Thomas's 'Do not go gentle into that good night'. It was not far off for him, the final one, and he was a fighter fierce and unrelenting. Standing up once, out of order, he had cried, 'While I'm on my feet I'll have my say' and I expect the lion roared.

I found his tombstone recently. Thomas Pollard. Died October 21st 1917. I wished I could speak with him, and tell him that his grandchild could also be fierce.

When one has forfeited ideas of survival after death the past becomes even more precious, and one begins assembling its treasures with respectful care hoping to give significance to as many short lives as possible, using them as a barrier against defeat, a gesture of defiance in the face of oblivion.

There was general concern about Mother's health which deteriorated: it was necessary she should have more air. A cottage fell vacant high up on Cliff-side right above the old Pollard home, and Father was able to take it.

Removals were fairly frequent in the village and carried out on hand-carts. Friends mustered to help, and a crowd of children tagged on behind, but since effects were neither numerous nor weighty, the operation was not long protracted. It was however interesting and revealing to those who were at all curious: someone's soul was out for an airing, its dimensions and quality displayed as if for a rehearsal of Judgement Day. A few proud spirits got the hand-cart moving at dead of night when the kindly darkness concealed either unknown treasures, or what was more likely, a paucity of possessions. We and our knick-knacks are one.

Up on the Cliff we were sandwiched between Miss Pearce above, and the Furses below. The Furses were Plymouth Brethren, and James Furse could have stepped straight out of Holy Writ. He had dark eyes, curly hair, a good voice and a fine presence. Annie, his daughter played the organ in the tabernacle, and Alfred her brother, a handsome daring enterprising boy with merry eyes, was captured from adolescence onwards by the special brand of orthodoxy practised by the Plymouth Brethren. Like all these sects it was a divisive influence, as far removed from Methodism as the latter from the Church of England or Rome. Alfred was as good as lost to his pals, a sad comment on human understanding.

Our sojourn on the Cliff lasted only about eighteen months. It was a perfect place for striking up an intimacy with the harbour, the quays and the bay, all there within arm's length. The serenity, the turbulence, the bustle, the brilliance, the silences, the depths, the colours and shapes and smells entered into your being. You communicated in the early morning, at mid-day, and when, the sun having left the sky, the waters gleamed darkly below. Those great cobblestones of the cliff road how blue they were and shining, and how saturated with heat the wall as you leant over it to gaze down into the sawdusty pit of Frazier's Yard.

Chapel Point, thrusting out its green arm on the west of the bay, provided a boundary of rest for the eyes. If our senses have been fashioned to seek after perfection, here the search is rewarded, and hunger for beauty assuaged. Green, slender and strong, and tapered with a splendid delicacy, Chapel Point lies on the water with a gentle grace that makes of the partnership a perfect delight.

It was while we were on the Cliff that World War I ended.

I was in bed with measles, Dollie too, and through the open window of our bedroom there drifted the sounds, slight at first, and then mounting to a roar, of the community preparing to celebrate victory. We were wrapped in blankets and taken by Father to the window to watch the excited noisy crowd pass up, bound for the Battery just round the corner from our house. The Battery is the flat topped piece of cliff whence years ago guns were fired at invaders.

In 1918 it was with intent to burn an effigy of the Kaiser that the crowd gathered. I'm very sure my father didn't take those few steps to participate in the ceremony. Burning effigies was not for him.

And so we entered the post-war world. By now Dick and Arch had started working and to Father's, their own and everyone else's surprise, they were very good at catching fish, and the old *Ibis FY 91* began to earn a name for herself.

Father found himself in possession of enough money, £400, to buy 17 Tregoney Hill.

III

School

The Infant School was 'up the Backlet' and the building is still there though not any longer used as a school. We began on the day we were four: the older ones had started at three. Father took each one of us when the day came, and delivered us into the hands of Miss Marfleet. It was 8th February 1915 for me, and I wore a bright red coat, and swallowed hard as I relinquished Father's hand.

The inside was dense with children all subdued, and the long badly-lit room had a gallery made up of steeply ascending forms without backs for support. Wedged in an inside corner of the top form you were quite securely imprisoned, tied down as firmly as any Gulliver, a thousand psychological pins fastening you to a regimen rigid and implacable. You were conditioned to an uncomplaining obedience, to a kind of infant serfdom where learning was the work due to an overlord. When years later I found Robert Owen in my history book, he became as much of a pin-up for me as any film-star. Accustoming ourselves to school must have been a Herculean exercise in adjustment for us, coming from a home so different. Father's head was all reason, and his heart all mercy, and Mother hardly ever finished shouting before she had begun laughing, exasperation melting into curiosity, irritation into hilarity.

Where or how they found our school mistresses I can't think. They came from afar, and reacted to the Cornish mentality with complete lack of comprehension. Miss Marfleet was a very strict woman indeed, but to give her her due, she did mellow with time.

I had been at school two years when Marjorie, the eighth

and last of our family, a delicate but spirited child, cherished the more because of her uncertain start in life, was delivered by Father to Miss Marfleet.

In an awesome silence we all answered a register in those days. For some reason, never discovered, Marjorie didn't answer her name. Reproved, she maintained silence, and what's more kept it up the next day. This was extremely serious, a piece of insubordination unheard of in that infant-adult world. It was necessary to treat such disobedience with stern measures.

I was sitting in that top corner already described. After registration our Marj, white and wide-eyed was dragged out into the centre of the pit below, and shaken in front of the whole school. Then she was shoved rudely into the small room adjoining, shouting filled the whole building, and I imagine penetrated the length of the Backlet. I was certain Marj would be executed and the horror that filled my frame is with me now. I should have rushed after the two of them, but was pinioned in the gallery.

In spite of the violence of this confrontation, there was still no response next day. Miss Ruby Craggs, Miss Marfleet's local assistant, and a gem of a teacher, came then to Father, told him of the 'trouble', and asked for his co-operation. So Father compiled a register of all our names, and gathered us round the kitchen table. He started with Mother, and worked downwards. We all answered 'Present' until he came to Marj. 'Father,' she said, 'I will answer for you or Miss Craggs, but not for Miss Marfleet.' Nothing more could be done! An impasse was reached. Confrontation and conciliation had both failed. Like so many of the insoluble problems of life, this had to be left to time for a cure.

One day Marj after severe toothache went to school with a swollen face; we called it 'felon'.

'Why have you come to school?' asked Miss Marfleet.

'Because I must,' said Marj.

Whereupon Miss Marfleet kissed her, and that day she answered her name.

Many years later, after Marj had started nursing, these two found themselves sitting next to each other in the St Austell bus, and entered into conversation. 'You know, Marjorie,' Miss Marfleet said, 'You were the only child who ever defeated me.'

We used to do a lot of oral spelling, and when the correct version was arrived at, up it went on the board writ large. The word was 'fruit'. Hands up. Yes, you. 'FRUTE,' I ventured eagerly. 'FRUIT,' murmured Jack Farran, controlled and correct. I had met with a masculine challenge! 'Ah yes,' I thought, 'of course, and Mr Farran has a lot of dried fruit in his shop.'

We danced the maypole in that small room. The ribbons were a patriotic Red, White, and Blue, and we used to sing a song 'Three cheers for the Red White and Blue'. The ribbons were smooth and strong, and it was exciting at first weaving the plait round the pole, and then unwinding, but the novelty passed and interest declined. It became a bit of a chore. This is the trouble with physical exercises and athletics in general. One gets bored with them. So much is repetitive and seems to lead nowhere unless competition, that vexatious element, is introduced. How many I wonder have the same feeling of sad deficiency in the matter which afflicted me as a child and still does?

There was a small yard made up of very large slate paving-stone into which we used to step out for a break, and that exit too was compulsory in all winds and weathers. The cold always paralysed me and a crowd rushing around in a small space brings me to a standstill. I remember crying miserably and weakly, congenitally incapable as I was of standing up to this sort of adversity. Dear Ruby Craggs came along and rubbed my hands, put her arm around me and led me into the lobby. Gratitude has a birthday for us somewhere.

Exit from school was a beautiful experience, tasted afresh morning and afternoon, winter and summer alike. You took away with you figures and words and snatches of song into the sunlight and empty spaces, and they germinated in your head and gathered to themselves a host of associations provided by nature herself.

You wandered home and Mother was always there: in summer the door stood wide open, and in winter the fire burned clearly in the kitchen range. If the wind was changing, there'd be an exciting saltiness in the air, and on the way down the street the smell of pilchards roasting on gridirons filled your nostrils. Always the seagulls wheeled and cried, fluttered and perched. Have you noticed what a graceful carriage the seagull has, with what an air of possession and pride it moves about in its own territory – along the edge of the quays, on the gunwales of the boats, and aloft on chimney pots? Beautiful the colours too, the silver sober grey and perfect white of the feathers, the brilliant orange of the beak, all to be found in the granite of the rocks where delicacy and strength combine.

'If only,' Dollie once said to me, 'these gulls would keep off my polyanthus flowers, silly creatures, beautiful, but dull-witted, and sillier the people who feed them.'

Woollen jumpers, home-done, were very much in fashion in our infant days, for happily there was no uniform for mothers to be worried with. True the jumpers got overtight with too much washing, and we almost all had experience of wearing shrunken clothes. I have seen children hanging by their jumpers grasped at the waist and turned inside out as if for removal. Then they were spun round with head concealed in the body of the garment, the tight neck preventing their being denuded quite. This kind of assault was the punishment usually for not being able to learn.

However, we were most of us quite secure at home, and nothing I have ever heard or seen in a state school has ever horrified me so much as the misery described by some of those educated in private and public establishments. How awful not to be able to go home at night, to think of parents being glad to get rid of you!

The aristocracy must be deficient in human feeling, insulated perhaps against love by a plethora of material benefits, or maybe diverted from the profundities of life by superficial attractions, rendered insensitive by a cocoon of wealth. Some years ago I visited a friend who had become housemistress in a boarding school where fees were high and prestige equally so. I was so sickened and depressed by the atmosphere I was glad to turn my back on the establishment and get home to the freedom and naturalness of a normal environment.

At seven we graduated to the junior department of the Board School. It used to puzzle me why it should be called Board, and I decided it derived either from the long dark boards of the desks at which we sat, or perhaps the blackboard. Education acts and boards of governors had not yet appeared on our historical horizon and black-boards were important as being the chief educational aid then devised. Standing on their easels, they obtruded clumsily into the limited space of crowded classrooms, but shunting them up and down, and jamming pegs into upper or lower holes provided a good channel for the exasperation, frustration and ferocity of tortured teachers. Board School gave its name to the precipitous hill which leads out of the village on the old road to St Austell.

One building, it had separate boys' and girls' departments, single sex education then being the fashion. The school-house is attached at the lower end, the great yew trees lending an air of solemnity to the whole. A high wall separated boys and girls, but noise in our time as now, knew no bounds. We were acknowledged with an infinite variety of sounds ranging from the friendly salutation to the bellicose yell. I cannot remember yard duty being done by teachers in those days – one blessing for them and us alike. Neither was there any need for us to be seen off at the gate, since traffic was light and harmless.

From the entrance hall I remember the heavy door on the left which led into the long room with windows facing south and west, but too high to look out of. This was the home of the headmistress and senior classes and served also as an assembly room for the whole school every morning.

A long passage full of coat-hooks divided this from the Junior Department on the right, a lofty cold place with the same high windows facing north. The middle school adjoined the big room on the left at the back, also with north-facing high narrow windows.

Not long before my time the headmistress had been a woman who hailed from the north. I knew her only by repute but she had scared my three older sisters and all their friends so completely that her name still spells TERROR for us all. For some time after she had left the grammar school Edith, my eldest sister taught as an assistant to Miss C. In consequence she became nervously ill, and the inevitable absence from duty only aggravated the situation. On poor Dollie's head was visited the wrath of this virago when Edith was away sick. Finally Miss C. was dismissed, for her harshness had become a public scandal. From this distance one cannot but be sorry for a poor woman who could never have known any happiness or peace of mind in this life. She was sick and misguided no doubt, and badly in need of the affection she could not inspire. It is the sadder that she should have been so wretched, and caused such misery in so beautiful a place where many of the girls were gifted and ready to respond to loving treatment.

I have read verses of Jennie Blamey, Sophie Rowse and Claudie Beswarick all twenty years senior to me, which prove that much talent must have lain dormant in crowded classrooms. Sophie, the singer who became Mrs Matta, and Jennie afterwards Dr Grier's wife, corresponded with each other in verse. They couldn't have been very old when nostalgically they looked back, Jennie writing.

We bathed in the sea at Portmellon,
In costume so very rare
Quite often in shimmering nainsook,
Not a part of us ever showed bare

and from Sophie:

The milk is brought now to our door
In foil-topped bottles bald,
I'd rather wander down Town Bridge
For a penneth o' Mary Kate's scald.

I imagine that the overriding emotion of us all at school was anxiety, and that long passages of time passed in joylessness. It was a razor's edge existence where at any moment you might topple into a pit of trouble. The high spirits, the resilience, the rosy expectations, the love of life peculiar to youth add up to such a powerful force that adverse circumstances must be severe indeed entirely to suppress it. Suppressed however it was, and substantially for a good many, above and below average alike. In confronting such a joyless area, the mind is baulked in pursuit of its memories, encountering a near vacuum where incident is thin, and surrounded by clouds of unease.

That delicate instrument which has to carry us through our lifetimes, suppressing the unpleasant, tries hard always to maintain a balance in favour of the happiness so necessary for sane survival.

How magnanimously right I have always considered A.S. Neill to have been.

Miss C. was succeeded by a Mevagissey woman Miss Maud Dunn, who had the difficult task of earning honour in her own county.

In the junior school I had Edith as teacher, and so did Marjorie for a short time later. It was an unsatisfactory situation, for Edith, trying and failing to be severe, was often stern with her young sisters, just to prove she was not favouring them, and since punishment was the rule, would sometimes use us as a safety valve. Poor dear Edith, she had a hard time of it, steering between the Scylla of a strict establishment, and the Charybdis of her own soft-heartedness and progressive ideas. Once quite unjustifiably, Edith gave Marj the ruler, (cane) and affronted and indignant, Marj went straight home and reported the matter to Mother, who when Edith arrived was exhorted by Mother to 'leave the cheeld alone'.

As for me, I got into trouble for quite unconsciously using Edith's Christian name, and on one occasion for not keeping awake. Working hard I became exhausted, and when discovered, my head on my arms fast asleep, was reprimanded, poked and derided.

Edith's health declined, and Father had the bold idea that she should go to college, an ambitious plan in those days. However it materialised and Edith was off to Exeter where she flourished and wrote long exciting letters to us every week. When she died in 1971 I found three letters from us in her box which she had kept since 1921. At eight Marj was writing:

> I dreamed last night that you were up to school teaching the girls and my other teacher was up there to. I am very sorry that I did not write you because I did not have time. I wish you were home now because I am longing to see you. Please Ede will you tell me when you write, please will you tell me my mistakes. Dear Ede this is not my best writing. One day Lily Burt had only one mistake in her dictation. from your loveing sister Marjorie to Ede.

and from me at ten years,

> My dear old Ede,
> How delighted I was with your lovely long letter, and it sounded comicle to hear you say There goes the tea bell for there is no bell home here to call us to tea. I hope it is not too swanky up there because when you come home you will be saying He'as a bit of meat father. You mustn't mind my writing as I am scribbling fast because I shall soon have to lay the cloth for dinner. We were just sitting up to table, and Doll told us about the man who had some manure in a bottle and how he did not carry the other kind of manure around with him, and how the boys did laugh. I think the little cough which the man gave made the boys laugh. Yesterday Miss Dunn walked into our room and told Miss Roberts that we were not to do part of our sums on paper. We did not get on at all nicely with our sums the first day she came in, but today we all finished them early. Now like Miss Roberts says I have exhausted all my little store so I must say Goodbye.
> Goodbyee, Don't syee, Theres a silver lining in the skyee. Bonswar old thing, cheere o chin chin La poo poddle de do. Goodbyee.
> From Mary to my old handsome Ede.

After Edith's departure there appeared Miss Mona Hunkin (a Mevagissey girl) and a Mrs MacMichael from Gorran. By this time I was in Miss Roberts's class. Marj adored Mrs

MacMichael, and used to push her bicycle up Tregoney Hill in the afternoons. She once told Mother how much she would love to give Mrs M. a present, and Mother turned out two new handkerchiefs, her private store, from one of the small narrow drawers of the yellow walnut wardrobe. Mona was very beautiful. She had black shining hair, a wide smile and a slow American-sounding husky voice. She wore a cream crepe-de-chine blouse amply cut, and fastened in front with one huge pearl button. Marj confided in me that she intended having a blouse just like that as soon as she grew up. Alas! the style went out of fashion.

The Middle School was neither more nor less than one person, a single lady, Miss Carrie Roberts, who became an institution, and whose sorry destiny it was to survive decades of teaching the young of her own sex in her own village. Weary circumstance in the shape of a monotonous existence beset her, but failed to erode her gracious manners, her perfect correctness, her lady-like demeanour.

Suppose she were to meet anyone of us in the village, perhaps dashing to get the St Austell bus, or jumping on to a bicycle to whizz down to Pentewan. 'Pleasant journey,' she would articulate very clearly, with a smile that engaged every muscle of her face, and revealed her beautiful teeth. Our names were enunciated with a muscial clarity, each syllable being given its due weight, every consonant its appropriate crispness. Dor-o-thee. Thel-ma, Mar-gar-ett, as if in scrupulous recognition of the components of our identities. Relentlessly she led us away from all that was slovenly, incorrect, or improper, into a world full of order, of culture, and most important, of refinement. Dear Carrie, she left her mark on the generations and there are many of us alive, and as many dead, who, could we be gathered together, would give a collective performance to prove how deeply that mark had been engraved on us all. She was poetical and patriotic, and recited in as rhetorical a fashion as Dylan Thomas himself. In fact I have become aware since I grew up what a great potential resided in that imprisoned spirit. Here now I must pay a belated tribute to her and include her with others and my own parents, of whom in a burst of emotion I once wrote:

In humble paths their honest footsteps trod,
Obscurity related to the name of God.

I found a photograph of her in Edith's box. She had given it
to my sister when the time came for Edith to leave for college.
It was her generous wish that her young friend should not
continue to suffer the sort of hardship to which she herself had
been subjected, and she wanted to lift the yoke of fear from the
shoulders of one whom she had loved as a pupil and a teacher.

Back to the classroom. There she stayed punctual and
ageless. She wore a voluminous black skirt which reached the
floor, and a decorative blouse with a high neck-band.

Her hair swept up at the back was arranged in a flat mass of
tiny artificially induced curls on the top of her head,
producing the effect of a wig, but I think it was her own thin
hair dressed in the safest manner possible and well-oiled. She
frequently sat on the desk with the ample folds of her skirt
wrapped round her legs, neat little feet (encased in winter in
black buttoned boots) sometimes protruding.

She worked very hard all the time, though a good deal of
wastage occurred through a nervous fussiness that reduced
her output. We were well grounded in the three R's, and the
syllabus included physical exercises, geography, history,
singing, sewing and art.

The geography was chiefly of Cornwall where Brown Willie
deputised for Everest, romantically remote, the Land's End
for the South Pole, and the Tamar for the Bering Straits. I had
an uneasy feeling we were being rather parochial, but human
values always counted more with us than academic progress,
and a bit of leisureliness was always welcome. We are an
unambitious race. There was a whole lot of large dusty maps
propped up in the corner, one of which would occasionally be
taken out and hung over the blackboard, only to fall down
with a clatter, just as if the map knew how useless was its
intrusion on to our geographical ignorance.

Sewing was a completely frustrating unproductive activity.
We made terrible garments in stiff white calico which
necessitated practising on a specimen for a year beforehand.
The Middle School process was fitting a gathered and

stroked piece of material into a band with tiny almost invisible hemming stitches. We did six stitches at a time and then queued up to have them inspected. In fact we became much more practised in queueing than in sewing. My stitches never once acquired the necessary regularity and I had to unpick them so many times that *six* large black holes in a blood-stained environment, left no nucleus of threads into which I could have another poke. I never produced the pinny or the chemise, which was the trophy one carried as a passport into the realms of upper-school needlework. I knew at the time how farcical it all was. (Children's judgements can be sound but I didn't bother to rebel.) Besides Miss Roberts used to allow a story during sewing, and often asked me to read aloud to the class which I loved to do, taking refuge in Hans Anderson from the tedium of craft. Background literature has since been superseded by background music.

Singing was chiefly learning notes in the form of Tonic-Sol-Fa from a chart imprinted with a myriad lines developing into cracks, which reflected its great age. Miss Roberts's style of conducting was of the flamboyant class, and she sang with us, throwing passion and pride into the performance. Doh was represented by a clenched fist thrown high in revolutionary fashion when the octave had been scaled. Do ray, Doh me, Doh Fah. Fah Fah Fah Fah (forefinger shaking) Doh Soh Lah Tee Tee Tee Teeee Doh. (Hold on girls, hold on.) It was an exercise conducive to hysteria. I once lost control, and let out a long rippling laugh when Miss Roberts's voice cracked, and was in disgrace for the rest of the day standing behind the board waiting for the solemn lecture which would be delivered after 4 p.m.

How many I wonder remember that splendid round we sang so often, jumping in firmly, and settling down quietly to a fair wind and warm sun:

Glide along my bonny boat
While with the tide we gently float
And chant to the deep seas' mellow note
Glide along
My bonny bonny boat.

We all left the classroom for the bay.

As for art we drew straight from nature, collecting wild flowers as subjects, germander speedwell, bird's foot trefoil and greater stitchwort. Miss Roberts favoured blackberries and ever-green aconite which grew in abundance at the bottom of Vicarage Hill in the region of the cemetery. She started us off with the skeletal architecture of the plant repeating over and over 'There's nothing stiff in nature'. Acting upon this dictum she made fine curved shapes of the straightest stems and branches. Our sense of the actual was seriously affronted by something so monstrously unrepresentative, but outrage has a way of melting into fun, and we were glad to manufacture any amusement possible. As always there were gifted children who went their own way, and Carrie was generous enough to recognise them, applying her dictum in praise of what obviously flouted her directions.

For physical exercises she dressed up well in cape and galoshes before taking us into the yard. I did the same myself years afterwards and successfully defied a formidable headmaster who could hardly believe his eyes when he found me in an old fur-fabric coat taking drill. I stared him out. We Cornish are not much for disciplines which demand daily monotonous exercises and a lot of repetition. We trust to adrenalin to equip us when the challenge comes.

I have been coursing around on the periphery of elementary education. The heart of the matter was the three R's and there is nothing wrong with that much-debated Trinity in the hands of a good teacher. Miss Roberts taught us fractions, and I can remember actually loving them, both the top-heavy improper ones, and the small proper ones standing alone or tacked on to whole numbers like children to their parents. What a thrill there was in the cancelling out process, reducing the cumbrous to the manageable, grasping intuitively the factors common to top and bottom, and rid of superfluities, producing a simple correct answer writ bold below. I have often wondered about the workings of mathematicians' minds and the vision which has led the great scientists to their discoveries. Pieces of Einstein's prose I have read with great reverence,

Enough for me the mystery of the eternity of life, and the inkling of the marvellous structure of reality together with the single-hearted endeavour to comprehend a portion, be it ever so tiny of the reason that manifests itself in nature.

We used to do a lot of mental arithmetic. The questions were numbered one to twenty daily. Quite early (aged about nine) I had to stand at the board and write up the initials of any girl who made a mistake and tack on the number of the sum. She would have to stay in from play to get all corrected, and I too to see that it was done. Well one day the rebel in me rose up against my overlords (Miss R. was under great pressure herself poor dear.) The sun was shining. I dropped my chalk and abandoned ship. When I got outside I realised I had committed a felony, perhaps the sin against the Holy Ghost whatever that mysterious piece of wrongdoing was, and having escaped one prison rushed into another – the lavatory. I crouched there shaken with fright at my own temerity. A crowd of girls gathered outside.

Soon Miss R. pushed her way through the crowd dispersing it as she approached.

'Mary, come out,' she cried, 'What would your father say, child? I'm sure your mother would grieve.'

'You're wrong there,' I thought, 'my mother would encourage me.'

It all passed off. The dear woman didn't report me to the headmistress but I was soon in harness again, a beast of burden, back in the old rut.

My heart still goes out to every oppressed 'worker' and when I hear the Red Flag a great surge of emotion overcomes me and my eyes fill with tears. We used to sing that hymn

When wilt thou save the people
Oh God of Mercy – when,
The people Lord the people
Not thrones alone but men,
Flowers of thy heart Oh God are they
Let them not pass like weeds away
Their heritage a sunless day
God save the people.

It was a sunless playtime in my case, but a perpetual dark night for those who didn't get their sums right, and could have been but small comfort when problems loomed large to hear 'I cannot get on; there's a straw in my way.'

As for English we seemed always to be writing dictation at a snail's pace. (In Standard 1 I lost a mark for writing a full stop in words.) We did Précis and compositions, The Lighthouse, A Penny's Adventures, Our Family, A Summer Morning and even had to tackle abstractions like Friendship and Loyalty. 'How well I remember the day that I was born,' wrote one girl outdoing Thomas Hood. 'It was a dull November day.'

Books were scarce, almost non-existent. There were a few single copies for teachers, sometimes their own property. We used to learn poems and passages of prose by heart and chant them as a chorus. For long years, for hundreds of girls the intonation remained the same, the pauses, the emphases, the allegros and andantes, so that a group of relatively old and young could repeat together poems and prose passages in identical voice and style,

> Breathes there the man, with soul so dead
> Who never to himself hath said
> This is my *own*, my native land
> Whose heart hath ne'er within him *burned*
> As home his footsteps he hath turned
> From wandering on a foreign strand
> If such there be *go* – mark him well

and so on.

Again in patriotic vein we pined for home with Browning: 'Oh to be in England now that April's there'. And (very brightly) whoever waked in England etc.

The novel for us all, year in year out was *John Halifax Gentleman*, which strangely enough is being televised as I write. We learned the first page by heart.

> 'Get out of Mr Fletcher's way, ye idle, lounging, little *vagabond*,' I think the woman Sally Watkins, once my nurse, was *going* to say, but, she changed her mind.

eft to right.
ddie, Father, Archie.
Taken to oblige

The Inner Harbour

Miss Carrie Roberts.
Teacher of Mevagissey girls for forty years.

An old corner in Mevagissey
Alma's materials on the step.

Mevagissey Post Office
In close touch with the Great World.

We got bogged down in the first chapter. Carrie seemed incapable of launching out into the tide of events; we were all dammed up in circumstance akin to that of our teacher's own uneventful life. However Edith sent me *David Copperfield* (unabridged) on my tenth birthday, and I was leading a double life taking thrilling private excursions into literature and living in another world.

Sometimes on still afternoons a pig would be killed in the field outside our window, that field immediately below Lavorrick Orchard recently ripped up for building purposes. The squealing offended Miss Roberts's sensibilities, and touched her tender heart. She always drew the blinds on these occasions and we sat in a subdued green light, which, though availing nothing towards the reduction of noise, induced even in the toughest some slight respect for the dying.

The straw hat in the photograph, or one very like it hung on a peg behind the blackboard near the spot where offenders stood with face to the wall. Dollie tells me that it was often donned by the bolder spirits of her group, and with nods and smiles they gave entertainment to the rest of the class, from a position, which, though taken up in disgrace was successfully adapted to purposes of theatre. Janie (Mrs Thomas) has reminded me of the particular form of chastisement that Carrie meted out. We held out a hand, and a pocket handkerchief well screwed up, was drawn briskly across it, the operation being accompanied by the solemn statement 'It's not for the hurt but the shame.'

At Christmas Carrie always gave us an orange each. The class was a big one, and an orange was a luxury in those days: she was generous.

We see her now tripping along, hand on hat, umbrella over arm, seeming scarcely to touch the ground as with a curious sideways motion she descended the steep hill. She moved daintily as a little yacht in a light breeze, when it skims over the water, tacking as it goes.

I wish I could think of her enjoying another better life, fulfilled and leisurely, for, like so many of the faithful she reaped a scant harvest in this one.

Carrie went home to Emma, an older sister, and Joseph

ET-E

Kitto (J.K.) Roberts, her bachelor brother. They lived in a long house in a lush garden as near to the churchyard as Haworth Parsonage to gravestones. Emma was a very brisk very attractive little lady, clever and social-minded. A member of the District Council, she enlivened local government with her good sense and enlightened attitude. J.K. was a builder and undertaker, and his premises occupied that piece of ground which, between the Bible Christian Chapel and the Buildings is converted into a car park. There's a telephone exchange there too.

A high wall broken only in one place for a green wooden door, surrounded J.K.'s orchard. Approached by a narrow lane, it was as mysterious as something from the *Arabian Nights*. The sun beat down not on sheets of metal as it does now, but rich brown earth, and apple, pear trees and vines which in season were loaded with fruit. (Carrie always used to eat a large apple during playtime.)

There was a peach tree too, and once when Father was ill I remember J.K. bringing him a peach, large and ripe. Father and J.K. were friends, between whom there was mutual respect, each one recognising the reasoned judgements, the intellectual integrity of the other.

I am in possession of an excellent little book by J.K.: *The Mevagissey Independents 1625-1946*. It was J.K.'s father who built the present Congregational Church. I am impressed by his love of history which he says has been described as 'the best tonic for drooping spirits'.

J.K. was busy with his studies while his sister coped with us farther up the hill. After two years we left the north-facing room and Miss Roberts, came into the top-class where reigned the headmistress Miss Maud Dunn, another local but younger woman.

Miss Dunn was tall and graceful, and would have been handsome had she been happier. A wealth of hair piled high on her head made her look taller still, and she moved with a light but very resolute step.

I realise now that she must have felt afraid, stepping into the academic world as into a foreign domain. It was necessary for her to make good: emancipated ideas had not filtered down into the remote elementary world of education and as we all know from personal experience and from literature it taxes the most patient and benevolent to live with children for a long unrelieved lifetime.

Miss Dunn's room was pleasant in itself, long and lofty; in winter the great tortoise stove glowed red, and throughout the year bright sunshine touched our heads from south and west in the mornings and afternoons. Mrs Williams, the caretaker kept it all spotlessly clean: everything shone, the long desks, the wooden floor the white walls, the piano, the table and Miss Dunn's high wooden desk. Joy was absent. It had not been part of the tradition in Mevagissey School, an emotion not associated with learning.

We were pleased to see Miss Roberts come in to play the hymn for morning assembly. I cannot remember ever singing any but two hymns. The first was 'My God, I thank thee who hast made the earth so bright,' which we droned to the pedestrian tune of Wentworth while Miss Roberts's fussy hands struck the tinny notes.

Having thanked God that joy was to be found in darkest spots we went on.

I thank thee more that all our joy
Is touched with pain
That shadows fall on brightest hours
That thorns remain.
So that earth's bliss may be our guide
And not our chain.

In Verse 4 we became engaged in close communication with the deity throwing fervour into lines 3 and 4.

I thank thee Lord that thou hast kept
The best in store;
We have enough yet not too much
To long for more.

The second hymn was 'New every morning is the love' and some of my readers will remember

The trivial round the common task
Will furnish all we need to ask
Room to deny ourselves, a road
To bring us daily nearer God.

I doubt if singing this every other day was inducive of asceticism in us; in any case rumours of the Russian revolution had penetrated as far as Mevagissey, and the more thoughtful of our elders were looking at things in an international context. Father was saying 'The world must be our parish'.

The content of that morning service and scripture lesson afterwards I never connected with the warm life of our chapel, the glories of creation, and the mystery of existence. It was part of the inexorable daily routine, encrusted with compulsion, a dreary piece of time to be passed with patience until the clock gave us leave to start arithmetic.

I sat in the back row just under that same clock whose hands so often seemed to stand still, almost arresting the circulation of one's blood. Janie Fulfit, one year older than me, and a veteran of the Senior School was my special pal. She took me under her wing, constituting herself protector, adviser, collaborator and friend. We worked together in that back row with great speed, and splendid conspiratorial accuracy concealed from Miss Dunn's piercing eye. Few words passed between us, since talking was forbidden, but our spirits were in harmony. 'Good maid,' she'd whisper, 'that's fine'. Janie had brains, personality and the kindest of hearts, but higher education was denied her. She is surrounded now by grandchildren who have inherited her keen intelligence.

Miss Dunn taught well and particularly arithmetic. I understood perfectly what she explained so clearly, and received that excellent groundwork which took me through Oxford School Certificate four years later.

Finishing my 'sums' by 10 o'clock I was the one to be sent by Miss Dunn to her mother's house in Back Street for the can of hot milk which was her mid-morning fortifier.

It was one of those milk-cans with a lid and a wire handle. I wended my way down Barbary's Lane (no houses there then) and drank in the summer sun, sucking a piece of grass, or singing to myself for sheer pleasure at being out-of-doors when everyone else was inside. A holiday is holy only when the rest of the world is working. Masses of valerian grew in Barbery's Lane, a bright companionable flower which I believe Quiller Couch loved and no wonder. I still associate it with the freedom and promise of brilliant Mevagissey mornings, and look at the vermilion spikes speaking almost in the hedge, with a nostalgia so overpowering that it threatens to burst the walls of my heart.

There was another excursion out from school on Mondays, this time down the hill and through the village to the bank with the bag of War Savings money. 'Trustworthy' girls took turns to perform this errand.

We used to bring our savings on Monday mornings anything from 6d to 2/6d according to the financial (or fish) times. It was then 15/6d unit which vanished into the fiscal system to become one pound in a distant future. Marj tells me she always dreaded the maturation of the unit because of the form that had to be completed. In fact she saw that 15/6d looming ahead for weeks an ominous amount, a dreaded dénouement. When a new card showed a sea of empty spaces it spelt reprieve from fear for enough time to relax.

What I remember best about that period in the top class is the arrival of visitors. Anybody was welcome as a distraction, a piece of entertainment. Once I recollect a governor coming through the heavy middle door, and descending the shallow steps he slipped and fell in a heap, his top-hat bouncing to one side, his umbrella clattering on the other. It was the fall of the mighty, the collapse of authority, an Act of God, and very funny. He wasn't hurt. Miss Dunn's solicitude was even funnier.

We enjoyed the visit of the school photographer though he wasn't given much time poor chap.

There was the occasion when Thelma Thomas arrived looking perfect, but she rashly decided to change her hairstyle at the last moment against Marj's advice. The result was a 'gaffing back' with creased ribbon and a flurry of wisps completely blotting out one eye in the photograph.

As for the inspector, when Miss Dunn got wind of his impending arrival, he was hung over us, an Itinerant Justice for a week-long anticipatory period. He represented the exposure of weaknesses, the rooting out of idleness, the disabusing of the confident, punishment for the cheat, and disgrace for the backward. As an inducer of dismay, dread and guilt he could not have been bettered. He was the law of the land, the dispenser of justice, the distributor of sanctions, straight from the highest seats of learning and legislation.

All scrap paper was banned, desks were tidied, inkwells washed, pencils sharpened, and nibs examined. In Miss Roberts's room there used to be a last minute wild scramble, a running round in circles, a superhuman effort to put on a good face. To this day I dislike inspectors, even the inoffensive kind on buses.

At last the great man stepped through the door. The long forms on which we sat squeaked on their hinges; we rose as one man, straightening bent knees and chanting 'Good morning, Sir.' We stood until motioned to sit. I needed the adjective 'ingratiating' before I could describe Miss Dunn's behaviour.

Sometimes the visitor would be an irate parent, even parents. The peculiar character of the knock on the door would send Miss Dunn rushing to open it and keep the intruder in the lobby. We heard raised voices in fierce conflict engaged no doubt in the dialectic of denigration, in the hurling of abuse accurately aimed.

Then it was over. The combatants had exhausted themselves. Miss Dunn returned: our wits and hers were wandering.

On occasion a very bold parent would burst into the room without knocking. This fairly shook the foundations of our adamantine régime: it can only be compared to one of those geological upheavals that brought the granite to the surface of Cornwall in some age or other. What terror, what pleasure in those moments full of a sort of exaltation compounded of freedom and justification. The young deal in the elemental with ease, the great potential in them rushing to invest whole areas of consciousness with magnificent world-shaking drama.

Then of course there would be the communication of the incident to Mother whose cryptic comments matched the alertness in her eyes, and the tension of her tilted head. 'Tell me the name,' she would say, 'and I'll tell ee the soort'. This was our first lesson in eugenics.

We didn't talk of these things to Father. Instinctively we knew that he would have nothing to do with a matter which was not open to impartial investigation. His probity was often too much for the tumultuous passions of our unfolding experience. He is still there for me inviting attention to all aspects of every situation, and counselling mercy for offender and offended alike.

Only once a year (apart from little tests) did we have examinations. I associate them with a profound silence, a new speedwell nib, a ruler and a piece of foolscap too splendid to deface. My great fear was of making blots, a frequent offence with me. It was as if some action painter operated with Stephen's Blue Black over my shoulder. What a high degree of unawareness and absence of intent can accompany our most serious malpractices.

The general attitude towards examinations has I think in some respects deteriorated in our time and become an obsession. Tests are for ever being blown up: I hate to envisage a society where certificates provide passports into a class of the meritorious producing a new form of élitism. Worth is hard to measure accurately and is subject to so many changes. Besides which, it flourishes most when its owner is so engrossed as to be unaware of it, rendering him independent of assessment. We think too much in terms of cleverness as something to be rewarded instead of a quality to be ploughed back into its source. Concerned so much with payments, we begin again to respect not so much the merit, as all the trappings that go with it. O Levels and A Levels obtrude everywhere, and degrees become attached to narrow-minded bores.

A.L. Rowse quite early came to the conclusion that genius was the only thing worth caring about. But surely genius, awesome and beautiful as it is, cannot be extricated from its social setting and what we must aim at is the greatest happiness of the greatest number, linking happiness with some fine quality of living which lifts it above survival and success, at the same time counteracting its brevity and pain. Genius for me can never be dissociated from an ethos embracing the whole of the human race whose great destiny it is to learn the lessons of justice and mercy.

May 24th was the only day we ever celebrated, an Empire date without import for the present generation.

We staged a tableau with the lower school only for an audience, and it took place in the back playground. First of all we marched round and saluted the Union Jack, while the heads of a few boys ('leaving the room' I expect) bobbed up over the wall, and a faint sound of jeering was heard as the snipers retreated.

Judging by the solemn faces in the photograph I have found, we must have had some foreknowledge of the approaching disintegration of the institution we were honouring. Roses, shamrock, leeks and thistles appear on the laps of pretty sober little girls grouped round Britannia holding her trident. Lolly Thomas's Indian turban had slipped out of place, just as the sub-continent did later, and she is trying to keep it up with her eyebrows.

In the meantime it seems that in the evolutionary ascent of man, Clive and Wolfe, Livingstone and Rhodes were regarded as nature's most splendid specimens to date.

Springs were warm in those days: the girls were almost all in white summer dresses except for me, and I appear as a very wan-looking John Bull, engulfed in a heavy overcoat, with a trilby concealing my forehead. Some imperialist producer had exploited my ability to learn verses, ignoring the fact that neither physique nor mentality qualified me for such a confident role. However, I couldn't be in possession of a better certificate of orthodoxy, and having been so obliging and uncomfortable in the cause of England on a hot day in 1922, I shall avail myself of this excellent testimonial, if anyone dares ever to accuse me of sedition.

There was of course the 'Scholarship' which loomed ahead for those who qualified and asked to take it. Many able children didn't apply. Either their parents were too harassed by poverty to entertain the ambition, or unconvinced that extra education would bring any attendant blessings.

It just happened for me. My parents were not importunate, nor inclined to overrate their children's abilities, although Father had great faith in education and believed it to be the best instrument for the effecting of the millenium. 1923 was my year. I went to St Austell with Peggy and others and sat in an upstairs room with a decent pen. The lid of the inkwell in my desk had stuck fast, and everybody else was well away before I got going. Mr Lodge, noticing my predicament, came along and slid it back for me. We had Précis to do, a splendid exercise which I have tried hard to teach in years past.

Does anyone else I wonder, like myself remember the clothes they have worn on special occasions, and only those? I had a bright brown light tweed dress made by Dollie. The round neck and hip-line belt were decorated with Russian braid in a deeper brown.

Coming back to Mevagissey, (it was sunny and mid-afternoon) I entered the kitchen where Mother was.

'Well and how did you get on?' she asked.

'Lovely,' I replied, hopping round on one leg.

'Ah,' she said turning her face away, 'you must fetch the bread now from the bakehouse.'

My mother was too pleased to dare show her pleasure. They were too accustomed to hardship and frustration ever to take any good fortune for granted, and even to feel confident now and then was to invite the disapproval of the gods. Successes great or small needed to be played down.

Our happiest times at school were in the yard where unsupervised, unregimented, untaught we organised our own games. Often we were there at 8.30 a.m. playing hop-scotch (hippety-beds, some round, some oblong.) Our stones we got from the beach the thin blue smooth variety and one with a sharp edge served as a tool to draw the beds. That in itself was a delight, constructing a clearly defined symmetrical shape, and doing it deftly and swiftly.

It was a satisfying game involving many skills, delicate footwork, good judgement of eye and hand, perfect balance, and overall precision. We played with the fierce concentration and complete absorption that spells dedication. The clanging bell was an ugly intrusion into a lovely world of lines and stones and special pals, a paradox of intense relaxation, an activity gentler, safer, more civilised and individual than team games, and your stone was as precious as a jewel.

Skipping came on with the colder weather, a splendid exercise for us all. We were light-weight children mostly, with plenty of spring in us. We used tarred rope from the loft and tied great knots to serve as handles so you see our games cost precious little. We played marbles too, lying on our sides in the sun.

Then suddenly there'd be a ganging up half against the school wall, half against the outer wall of the yard. 'The wolf has gone to Devonshire so Run, Run, Run.' Devonshire was a realistic representation of remoteness. I was never much for action in the mass and became an observer. It was a happy playground with few squabbles. I think we must have been good children, like the majority of young things when they aren't harassed.

And then came the end of term, when as many children as there were geranium plants in the window were saddled with a pot to care for throughout the holidays, a nuisance disguised as a mark of trust. Marj has told me how anxious it made her lest she should one day forget the watering, or that some other accident should befall the school geranium. Tom Tulliver's rabbits had likewise been too much for Maggie.

Finally there supervened the summer holiday, five long glorious weeks, wherein unmeasured time allowed the putting to sleep of apprehension, and tomorrow and tomorrow ushered in only happy days. It was a kind of rehearsal for heaven, an eternity, a sunny, salty, sandy, seaweedy, barefooted paradise. Ah! What glory! How good it was to be alive! So exciting and intoxicating was the freedom. What fortunate children we were to live in such idyllic surroundings, our very own and undefiled. Emerging from school in July, such deep thankfulness welled up in us as made a serious emotion of our joy, and had we burst into song, it would have been to give a grand slow moving rendering of the Doxology.

IV

Wesleyan Methodist Chapel

Our Wesleyan Methodist Chapel was the largest of four Non-Conformist buildings in the village, only a few yards from the harbour and next door to the King's Public House. It was a large well-built lightsome place with an air of grandeur about it, and not until recently when it was demolished did people realise it should have been conserved for its architectural value.

For us it was a second home, its ecclesiastical veneer but thinly disguising a secular almost domestic atmosphere. We gathered as a community not only to worship, but to exchange greetings and find security in the presence of friends.

For myself I could never have defined sacredness: It was a matter of the everyday world being unaccountably touched with glory every now and then. The poetry of the Bible had much to do with it for it seeped into our working days. Life stretched ahead, a sun-drenched eternity, its end a Judgement seat without terrors, for we were not cradled in fear, and superstition got precious little hold on us. I very early dispensed with God as father, being quite content with an earthly one who supplied all my emotional needs. Outside the tall clean windows of the chapel seagulls wheeled, indifferently remote from dogmas and creeds.

The chapel was often full on a Sunday evening, and always so on special occasions. The singing then swelled into a sweet and mighty sound, a great ocean of harmony, and God could have been in no doubt that it was Anniversary Sunday or perhaps Harvest Festival. One minister, the Reverend Ernest Picken, when first he heard that sound, was so startled, so over-powered with delight that he said he seemed to stand at heaven's gates and wept with joy. He was a sensitive creature, with large grey eyes in a long sad face. Wearing a shabby coat with the elbows out he would appear at our kitchen door and enter as if to his own home. It was his pleasure to sit there and watch my mother making pasties. His wife, a tall beautiful lady, very scholarly, had been the headmistress of a missionary school in India. Her fair hair, blue eyes, long legs, and cultured voice entranced us. So lovingly deferential was she to her fellow creatures and in particular the young, she charmed them into feeling royal.

There came a baby girl to the Pickens, and I used to spend whole mornings at the Manse keeping mother and daughter company. I watched the bathing and was most impressed to see Mrs Picken describing her baby's reactions to soap and water in a notebook. I reported this activity to my mother who looked into the far distance and then turning her gaze on me said it was due to the lady being educated, and I must on no account remark or show surprise at this or any other strange phenomenon. Some years later that little girl, beautiful and clever, died from an infection when visiting Cornwall on holiday. Tragedy has different components for all of us. Mary Barla's death was the experience from which grew my realisation of all that is agonising in life.

There were three ministers in our circuit who took many of the services as they still do. The quarterly plan was pinned in a prominent place in Methodist homes, but in ours it resided in the sideboard drawer where it was often buried amongst secular literature.

The preaching force included stronger and weaker brethren, some educated, others unlettered, a few brisk and pithy, and as many verbose and flowery. My father laid it down that we should always be present when one of the weaker variety was operating. Unfortunately the feebler the sermon, the longer it was apt to go on.

We entertained the preacher to dinner and tea quite frequently. There was one slow-speaking deliberate gentleman from St Austell who looked like Jesus himself, and whom we were not long in classifying as a member of the Wodehouse species of hypochondriac. He used to take a rest on Sunday afternoons, and repaired to the upstairs sitting room where the blinds were drawn at his request. One or other of us would almost always forget and crash into the darkened room. Another was a vegetarian for whom a special dish was prepared. The boys eyed his plate furtively, between bites so to speak, regarding this renunciation of flesh as a monstrous piece of eccentricity. When Mr W. praised meatlessness they smiled broadly and a heavy foot would be brought down on the opposite number under the table. They had been warned to say nothing contentious or disparaging, but smiling silences can speak volumes of incredulity and outrage.

A third St Austell guest was a very soft-spoken refined gentleman who once asked me how I liked Shakespeare. I shall never forget the look of pained surprise on his face when I announced a preference for Rider Haggard. (I was immersed in *She* on that very Sunday). The acute sensation of blunder suffered at that moment I associate with my farewell to childhood, to honest statements and too spontaneous rejoinders. Alas, I fear that along with others of my breed I have never properly learned the lesson of adulterating strong opinions. We still deal in solecisms as part of our stock-in-trade.

In the pulpit there were superb and highly individual performances. We had no theatre in our lives as such, but chapel provided us with as much drama as the most advanced of modern educationists could demand. My eldest sister, Edith Jane, and brother Dick, both excellent mimics delivered pulpit oratory regularly at home for Mother's benefit in Father's absence. He forbade what he called mockery whereas Mother despite her threats that we'd 'all be catched up in the moon' was waiting for the entertainment she hadn't received at first hand. I can see her now catching up the end of her wrapper (apron), throwing it over her head and crying, 'For shame, for shame.' Then with a sustained ripple of the most infectious laughter she would peer out, her dark eyes all alight and invite the same again.

One of the subjects was a Gorran man who really delighted in life and the gospel. His rather neutral sermons were accompanied by a strong regular rhythm produced by a flexing of the knees and a vigorous stretch to stand on the toes. Dick's name for him was Spring Mattress. He was a cut above the working man, wore a tweed coat, and was neatly groomed. The springing diverted attention from anything he had to say, and was as good as any Slumberland bed for relaxation purposes.

At one time there were no fewer than three of the staff of St Austell Grammar School on the plan. The eldest of this trio appeared in the pulpit as a transformed personality. At school he played a passive role, where, glued to his desk, he acted in a purely consultative capacity. We did about as much consulting as, medically speaking, the poor did before the time of Aneurin Bevan.

Dispensing the gospel, this remote figure came alive, reading the notices he once announced the subject of a midweek talk as being 'Outside the Pale' '*But*' he added, 'you must know it is PAIL.'

In contrast to the intellectuals from the realm of higher education we had simple untutored lecturers. One was short, square and very dark with large black eyes and curly hair going thin.

Like Billy Bray he was one of those who had been converted from recklessness and abandon to rectitude and righteousness. (Mother described such as 'a bit of a reprobate at one time'). He would literally hang over the pulpit and with his right arm on the left side of his mouth speak in confiding tones to us as individuals, fixing first one and then another with his great black eyes, 'My dear friend,' he would enquire, 'are you saved?' There was a strong current of magnanimity in his nature of an older date than his conversion. Dear fellow, if he was a blacksmith, he certainly succeeded in forging our very strong affection, causing us great mirth at the same time.

The most famous of our locals was a Mevagissey man Johnny G. who could neither read nor write. He had laid to heart long passages from the Bible which he delivered in a voice ranging from a whisper to a roar. The tempo was as various; nothing at Stratford was ever more impressive. Moreover the subject matter was poetically imaginative, often topical, and full of the most surprising metaphors.

When the aeroplane first appeared he envisaged God as a traffic warden, in the sky directing its passage among the indigenous angels, and preventing clashes. The air became thick with machines and winged spirits and God was verily distraught with the responsibility of it all.

Johnny liked to think of himself as a missionary travelling afar and taking the gospel to the heathen in foreign lands. When it came to specifying which people and what habitat we discovered he was describing the denizens of the St Austell Clay District known in Mevagissey as the Higher Quarters. Surely it was William Cowper who spoke of a less interesting species travelling the world over without their imagination being touched.

Johnny was in hearty agreement with his Master on the obstructive nature of wealth in connection with access to heaven. The rich could expect no passport. He once said it would be harder for one of Mr So and So's cows to walk up Polkirt Hill backwards, climb a tree and cavee (have a calf) in a bird's nest than for a rich man to enter the kingdom of heaven.

The grades of society he described in terms of door-knockers. The top-class were Brass-knockers, the middle Iron and the low No-knocker grade, but imagination led him through door of brass and iron, and with powerful percipience into the psyches of the more privileged inmates.

We chanted Gray's Elegy at school and remember 'Some heart once pregnant with celestial fire'. Such was Johnny's, but 'the general current of his soul' was not frozen, neither was it 'a desert air' on which his sweetness fell. Sweet were his daring metaphors to our ears, and before we had finished chuckling, his 'noble rage' had been imparted to us. There is more than sentimentality in Gray's Elegy, indeed yes.

Once a quarter the collection was for the Horse Hire Fund, which took local preachers to their respective destinations. They enjoyed their day out. It gave them a chance to put on 'their bit of best' to admire the country, to get things off their chests in the pulpit, to see and talk with fellow-Methodists abroad, and as well to have somebody else's good dinner. One famous Mevagissey local, eloquent and gregarious used to visit other homes after the service before going to dinner at the appointed place. Once, visiting a neighbour he saw a chicken taken from the oven and said 'Well now my dear, I might as well stay here today, they won't mind next door.' Alas, the chicken was taken out of that door and into the next one. It was humbler fare our friend had as a reward that Sunday.

Talking of collections there was one for the Education of Ministers' Children. My Grandfather Lakeman strongly objected having to educate anybody else's children while his own remained in a state of deprivation. On one occasion he dropped a half-crown into the baize lined box mistaking it for the mean penny he intended subscribing. His consternation was great when he discovered his mistake and he asked my father, who was a steward, to recover the coin. Father firmly replied that the mistake was irreparable, and that he would on no account try to do any such thing.

The season came round for a visit from the evangelist. Some force had to be brought in from outside to gain recruits for the faith, to save souls for the Lord. The even tenor of our days was interrupted, our regular routine disturbed, and our self-sufficiency challenged. To many of us it was altogether superfluous and unpleasant, an intrusion on our privacy which distressed and dismayed us, and a threat to the peace which suddenly became so precious.

There was only one evangelist that I distinctly remember. He was a tall florid man with very white hair and a confident stride. So few were the visitors to our village in those days we recognised him well before Sunday came. I was already busy building up a firm resistance, in fact positive opposition to this saver of souls from the time his coming was announced. My inner life was my own, a domain which only great friends were allowed to enter, and I was determined it should remain so.

> The soul selects her own society
> Then shuts the door.

Marjorie was seized with a terrible frightened distaste and on meeting the gentleman in the street ran home as fast as she could go and hid her face in Mother's skirts.

There was no escaping attendance. I sat with dread awaiting the appeal for conversion and praying to my own God that I should not capitulate. Neither did I. That border had been violently crossed where the search for truth, and concern for humanity are swamped by love of power, where the ego romps on regardless of its impertinent trespassing.

Old and young reeled towards the communion rail. Marjorie asked Mother if she should join them. 'No,' Mother said, 'Sit still, it will soon be over;' Father was very withdrawn and sad-looking at this time. I was too young to talk to him about it and we all suffered from acute embarrassment, but I believe Father was afflicted by a powerful sense of guilt that he hadn't even joined the Church. It wasn't until I was much older that I came to know of his doubts and attendant scruples, and I have ever since resented the power that religion in certain guises possesses to make sensitive creatures miserable, as if they must be punished for their very goodness, their integrity and honesty.

Because of these same doubts, Father never contributed anything at Prayer Meetings held on occasion after the evening service. True such prayers provided a channel for self-expression and must have relieved many pent-up fears, anxieties and sorrows. Our friend Lisbeth Chesterfield has told us that the most fervent prayer she ever prayed was, 'Lord, let not father pray.' Cap'n Charlie was a favourite with us. Perhaps an even more fervent prayer had often been 'Give us this day our daily bread' an earnest entreaty which the desperate hoped that the Wesleys' God would take literally.

I have already mentioned the singing at Anniversary Services. I suppose we need anniversaries to help us make some sense of the flux of time, to bend it into some shape wherein we can fit our own small portion. How else could we build up a pattern of any significance?

At one time the arrival of the evangelist coincided with Sunday School Anniversary, an arrangement we deplored and resented. Who was the kill-joy we wondered out to spoil our fun? This was a splendid early summer occasion demanding new clothes in which we would sing to crowded houses. Such an intrusion didn't happen a second time!

We were issued with leaflets on which were printed the words and music of special tunes. They just drifted into our hands. I wonder now who wrote them and where they came from; some Wesleyan warehouse? The rhythms were strong, the tunes full of runs and repeats. A few practices and these ephemeral airs had insinuated themselves into our heads. Escaping into the pure clear light of early summer they became associated with the smell of new mown hay.

Practising under Mrs Evelyn Rowse was rigorous: the trebles had a way of becoming too strong, and altos in second row needed fortifying. As for the anthem that was a most ambitious undertaking, a great test of the organist's judgement and our collective ability. How well it would stand up to the performance of the Bible Christians was the great question. My father occasionally expressed a few doubts about the ethics of the musically-endowed. 'It seems to me,' he said, 'they are far too competitive and given to contention. Quarrels have a way of beginning in the choir.' He was rendered immune from infection by a total absence of any ear for music.

The Sunday School gave a Cantata in the afternoon, sitting on seats erected in the space between pulpit and Communion Rail. I remember once being given the lead, and the tune in two sharps which took me up to 'g' is still in my head. Dollie, full of enthusiasm and ideas, made me a white voile dress with an embroidered scalloped hemline, and I wore a wreath of flowers in my hair. Happy days!

Later on came Harvest Festival when nets were draped over the gallery avoiding the clock-face (not all preachers had watches in those days!) and displaying the occasional fish trapped in the meshes. Anchors too hung over the rails symbolic of our anchorage in Christ. 'Will your anchor hold in the storm of life?' Haven't most of us felt it give?

The quantity, variety, and quality of the produce never failed to astound and delight us. There must have been many with an aesthetic sense far too strong for any puritanical creed to stifle. Blue skies and fertile fields were the reality and triumphed over the theology of the Wesleys. It was interesting to speculate from whose gardens the beautiful fruit and vegetables came and who had contributed the grapes rare in those days and chiefly black. A whole range of apples was displayed, the like of which we never see now, Pollies yellow and sweet, Lady Sutleys and Longnoses (Stubbits, Mother called them) which grew in Mr Smitham's Valley Park Orchard. The smell that filled the chapel compounded of apples and chrysanthemums was superior to any incense and equally intoxicating. It brought out the pagan in us always near the surface. This was a Festival of Pantheism and Polytheism ousting the Hebrews quite.

As for the Sale on the Monday evening, Sotheby's has never drawn a more determined crowd. Bidding would become abandoned and marrows like works of art acquired values as preposterously high as the bravado of competing purchasers was desperate. Then it was all over for another year, twelve long months, an eternity to the young. I could never understand why the old harped so on the brevity of life, but know now how much it resembles the shortest strangest dream, John Donne's 'prison-house through which we pass to our execution', and where sometimes the dream develops into a nightmare.

Some members of our chapel I must mention by name. Mr Peter Moore was an important trustee. Tall, dark, pale-faced, black-eyed, he wore a drooping moustache and a long black overcoat to match. Suffering from deafness he spoke with his ear cupped in his hand, and made weighty utterances balanced by a twinkle of the eye. He was great on church management, organising the big days and interviewing ministers, and I imagine he venerated John Wesley next to God, perhaps extending the Trinity to include him. He called Father Richard, and took his approval for granted. Mr Way, also a Trustee, was short, neat, lean and keen; his rosy complexion contrasted well with his strawyard boater and he sang with gusto, hymn-book raised high, 'Master speak thy servant heareth.'

Richard Martin Lelean, genteel and soft spoken was the predecessor of Mrs Rowse at the organ. He and Mrs Lelean sat in the pew immediately in front of us, a perfect pair benign and blameless. Mrs Lelean had fine nut-brown curly hair which fell over the collar of her cape at the back, and her handkerchief was perfumed and edged with lace. She was George Eliot's Nancy Cass, elegant full of grace and rectitude, and like Nancy, childless. She smiled on us with a sweet sadness.

Johnny Libby taciturn and grumpy, sat in a side seat near the door. Once upon a time, impatient with a latecomer who had let in an unwelcome cold draught he shouted, 'Shut that dooer.' His imperious gruff voice reverberated through the building during one of the pauses in the first prayer. It was strange the way that the foibles of our congregation had a way of coming to the surface never securely contained in the sacredness of the proceedings.

Another dramatic moment was when a visiting notoriety on a special occasion in a full house remarked on Mr Sam Furse not having removed his black bowler, and publicly censured such an act of disrespect for God's house. Sam, whose head had always been quite bald, never left off his hat in public, and the bowler was as much a part of his organism as anyone else's hair. Father, horrified at the rudeness and pettiness of this insensitive cleric, and trembling with sympathy for his embarrassed mortified friend, got up, shy and retiring as he was, and in a firm clear voice said, 'Sir, there is a very particular reason why our friend does not remove his hat. No disrespect is intended. Please excuse him.'

Mr Willie Furse and Mary Jane his wife were real stalwarts, part of the fabric of the place and always there. It was as if they and their pew were one. The Furses all had a certain dignity about them, and walked with a glide. Mary Jane, a great critic of sermons, and indeed of looks and clothes, gave judgment in a gruff bass voice.

Cap'n Pollard (Edwin) and Mrs (Emmie) attended when at home from sea. Very prosperous and handsome, they brought with them a foreign more sophisticated world. Cap'n was Mother's first cousin, and appears elsewhere in my story. I think they must have been home from sea to encourage and contribute to the redecoration of the chapel. It was done in pink and blue and at the same time we sported new brown velvet cushions for our pew, soft and comfortable, and so plum. They boys must have had a good catch at the time they were ordered.

Miss Beeby, and Miss Winifred Evans sat well up to the front. Miss Beeby was an outsider who had become naturalised. She had a private income, lived in the Georgian house on Polkirt Hill, and adopted Dr Barnardo's as her pet cause. She suffered from a cleft palate, and our Edith mimicked her quite perfectly, combining the exact sound produced by this disability with the very pious content of Miss Beeby's conversation. Mother was pretty sure that one day Edith would be 'struck' (she wasn't) but joined with us in laughing until we all cried. Miss Winnie Evans a local girl became Miss Beeby's companion and her eyes were as large as Miss Beeby's were small. Winnie was clever and should have had an academic career. She worked hard all her life for the Red Cross, and in the end was decorated at Buckingham Palace. I met her years after Miss Beeby had died, attending a WEA Poetry Course at Balliol College.

Adolescent boys broke away from their seats in pews downstairs and sat in groups in the gallery. We girls graduated to the choir second row first, and front row perhaps later. We were more interested of course in the population of the gallery than the pit. Ecclesiastical vestments, unknown in Non-Conformist circles, provided no help in concealing the natural creature. Which reminds me that amongst the clothes mass-produced for men in those days was a dark navy velour-cloth overcoat with a narrow velvet collar.

It happened that Johnny Dunn and Father had each chosen such an overcoat at the same time.

Dollie, coming out from evening service in the dark took the arm of an overcoat, and it wasn't until she reached the bottom of Tregoney Hill that she discovered she was walking not with Father but with Johnny. In his kindliness and wisdom dear old Johnny, always obliging, had not thrown her off.

Chapel like Sunday School had to celebrate its origins and development so another anniversary there was in the fall of the year. Special services were held on the Sunday and a great congregation attended filling every seat and overflowing into surrounding spaces. A 'fine' preacher was invited, special music well rehearsed and appropriate hymns chosen for community singing. There was a great sense of occasion, a powerful feeling of solidarity. We fortified ourselves against the dangers of existence and drew a loving God into our circle as a sure defence.

I remember particularly

Our Father by whose servants
Thy house was built of old
Whose hand hath crowned thy children
With blessings manifold
For thy unfailing mercies
Far strewn along our way
With all who passed before us
We praise thy name today.

Tommy Rowse, Martin Chesterfield, Dick Hunkin and John Warren rendered splendid quartets with wholehearted zeal and great sweetness.

My sister will sometimes sing to me as they sang to us

In the days of my trouble I cried unto the Lord
And he delivered me from all my sin.
Therefore will I praise him, etc.

We were all redeemed and made whole, and what a good looking man was Martin. Then Sophie (Matta) sang solos in the manner of an opera star outstripping in her untrained purely natural fashion the performance of the great Melba herself. In fact Sophie was Mevagissey's Melba. She was Tommy's sister. Tommy's wife Evelyn was the organist who had passed all the examinations and was really proficient. Myra Ball sometimes deputised for her, and Myra like her namesake Myra Hess had music in her soul.

The sermon was awaited when oratory would have its turn. We soared to the heights this time on a philosophic scale now in a major, now in a minor key. When the benediction was pronounced dispersal was accompanied by whispers only.

A few years ago my brother Dick, sister Marjorie and I

attended a service in Stornoway on a September Sunday morning. We sat in the gallery, and recaptured there something we thought we should never experience again. This time though we were half spectators viewing objectively something which had once been a vital part of our lives.

On the Monday following the anniversary, Chapel Tea was held in the Sunday School. It was a splendid starch meal and the cakes made on the premises by a band of experts. My sister Dollie was at one time responsible for the ordering of ingredients and still has the notebook in which she entered amounts required. She had to be careful to give equivalent orders to all the Wesleyan shopkeepers. I remember popping my head round the door to have a peep at the huge bowls of flour, pounds of farm butter, bags of sugar and fruit ready washed and dried. There was a batch of saffron and another of white yeast dough. They also made black soda and sweet seed cakes and golden bread and splits.

It isn't nostalgia only that renders the memory of that tea ambrosial: it was food fit for the gods and eating it you felt that all men were brothers. Rich and light the yeast cake was, the splendidly risen dough supporting an ample quantity of currants and sultanas evenly throughout its bulk. The crisp crust had the picturesque roughness of a relief map. As for the soda cake it was of a flavour and texture of such excellence as made of it an inspired mixture.

There was a Chapel Tea joke about the necessity of bringing an umbrella to the table into which to drop samples of cake. Someone had evidently used hers as a receptacle on a time.

To come back to the preparation. About a week beforehand the yeast dough was 'wet-up'; put to rise and when 'plum' lightly tossed into strong shining two-pound tins. It went to Mrs Rowe's bakehouse by appointment and was fetched back to the Sunday School, and given a few days to set. There's a souvenir shop now on Victoria Square where the bakehouse stood. A great melancholy assails me as I pass by the modern window.

On the afternoon of the Monday two coal-fires blazed in the Sunday School grates, and bowls of chrysanthemums glowed with similar warmth. Everyone dressed up for the occasion. Cornish people love clothes and bright colours. The men wore their best suits and ties to contrast with their dark complexions: the women came in their winter-coats with hats to tone. There was a wonderful feeling of expectation in the atmosphere.

Outside the winter sky was lofty, and the salty air deliciously crisp. Soon the herring season would begin and we were in anticipatory mood. Life was good: why should fortune not favour us? The future must unfold some glory of which this celebration was a foretaste. Ah! What a splendid thing is youth, how generous its calculations, how full its heart of trust and hope, Dear innocent youth!

The memory is very clear to me of those long trestle tables running parallel at the inner end of the Sunday School, the forms jammed with every variety of God's creatures, all Wesleyans.

The tables were covered with long strips of white calico. (Every family of any substance provided one). The feast was so arranged that all had access to the whole gamut of delicacies. Splits were lavishly buttered, cake cut in oblong pieces; doyleys were crocheted – no such thing as paper coverings in those days.

The aged and the infants sat cheek-by jowl, great grannies, toddlers, granfers and juveniles, mothers, fathers (never mums and dads mark you) sons proper, and sons-in-law, a host of relatives legal and not so legal, their names all entered in the parish register. You were identified by 'the cut of your jib'.

I studied the faces of some whom I loved, neighbours and friends, faces of the old, worn and seamed, their eyes clouded over, and mouths trembling, bewildered sweet smiles forming and vanishing in the same instant. At least they were secure in the bosom of their families, and if the fear of death was even then visiting them, they knew that a loving arm would steer them along that lonely road, the arm perhaps of a grandchild or a nephew with a special feeling for his single aunt. If 'the sands of time' were not yet sinking for us, we sometimes were visited with intimations of mortality, and a strand of pain ran through the fabric of youthful delight, brought to consciousness by an involuntary tear.

An important winter feature of chapel was the Wesley Guild, a group open to all ages from about 14 years upwards which met on Friday evenings. (No homework to do.) We sat up at the end near a large coal fire and our minister took the chair. Mr Picken always encouraged contributions from our own members who gave talks or read papers. Quite often we'd have a visitor.

Howard Dunn, Fish Buyer, County Councillor, St Austell Grammar School Governor, a progressive in politics and religion, friend of the people, reckless, outspoken and democratic, never refused to help us out. His Cornish voice was very near to the American in accent. He talked sense and we loved him, but often he failed in communication, and had recourse, in the absence of the right substantives to a lot of 'wot ee coll its.'

One evening when he was particularly inarticulate, four or five of us sitting in the front row were taken with the giggles, so that watching us, at first sternly, Mr Picken finally lost control and burst out laughing himself. I can see his expressive long face now alight with sympathetic mirth.

Sometimes a grammar school master from St Austell would come. Remember we had no radio or television then and were glad of any entertainment. Mary Jane Furse read Cornish yarns in a very rough voice, and then someone would sing a solo, or play on the tinny piano. You could break down with impunity in those days and start again without embarrassment. How much healthier it was than the inflexibility which now so often accompanies professionalism. I can think of a few stiff-necked who have lost their humanity in their perfection.

Now again the quartet (already named) would contribute an item. The most startling piece they ever sang was 'Man, Man, Man for woman was made.' Now in the audience that evening sat our Mother and Mrs Way together. They were then in the late fifties, and had borne long families, were alike in being thin and worn, having very bright eyes and a lively sense of humour. Sex had certainly not been a neglected activity in our village: in fact there were few other diversions, but it was never never never mentioned in public. Imagine the consternation battling with delight in those two when four impeccable young men spouted those daring words in tenor and bass from full throats in a Methodist Sunday School. Marjorie says she'll never forget their reaction, the shaking shoulders, the bowed heads, the spluttering *and* choking, with hands over mouths and handkerchiefs to eyes. It was all something to do with Genesis that might have, but didn't cause an Exodus!

At one time I gave a paper myself on Emily Bronte whose wholehearted devotee I had then become. In the front row were several middle-aged ladies amongst whom I believe was Mrs Robins who approaching 100 is still alive at the time of my writing. Mary Jane Furse was there too. With adolescent ardour I spoke of Emily's great genius, beauty and fortitude, her devotion to her Papa, Branwell and sisters, her fierce independence, wild imagination and proud secrecy. I claimed the Brontes as relations of ours. Was not Penzance a stone's throw away? As the fire sank in the grate I concluded with 'The Visionary', and we heard the rustle of an angel's wings.

> What I love shall come like visitant of air
> Safe in secret power from lurking human snare;
> What loves me no word of mine shall e'er betray
> Though for faith unstained my life must forfeit pay!
> Burn then little lamp glimmer straight and clear –
> Hush a rustling wing stirs, methinks, the air;
> He for whom I wait thus every comes to me,
> Strange Powers! I trust thy might; trust thou my constancy.

There were tears in their eyes as I finished. 'Ah my dear, that was lovely,' they said. How much they loved and needed poetry and more poetry. No word of approval from the academic world has ever been sweeter to me than that simple heartfelt expression of appreciation from Mevagissey grandmothers. Sometimes over the years I have half-suggested to friends that I adopt a sentimental attitude towards the working class modelling it on early experience of a breed which no longer exists. Seizing the bait, they have been ready to agree, at which point, in true Cornish fashion I have risen up undaunted and in the spirit of Emily thundered out my loyalty. 'Though for faith unstained my life must forfeit pay!' We aren't exactly easy to deal with, we Cornish.

As was our wont, we sisters walked to the end of the quay after our hour with Emily, and gazed out over the heaving waters gleaming darkling under the starlit sky with the little lights of the village burning behind us. Perhaps some of my readers will have become acquainted with Winifred Gérin's *Life of Charlotte Bronte.* If so they will remember Charlotte's great delight when first she saw the sea.

Another paper I remember being read by our brother Archie. He was of a literary turn of mind and was then assembling the works of Dickens in blue binding with gold lettering. The title of his paper was 'Are Second Thoughts Best?' and it went down well. Some time afterwards one of the family found an article of the same title in a Canadian magazine posted to us by some emigrant cousins living in Montreal. Trust a sibling for uncomfortable discoveries. Poor Arch, how he was ragged. He hadn't stolen much except the title, but he had to pay for it, and since he was so good at ragging himself needs must take plenty in return. 'Hadn't you better think again brother?' or 'Have you had any first thoughts, old chap?'

There were Wesley Guild Outings as far afield as Bude and Clovelly to the north and Penzance to the west. After Laurie Lee's matchless description of a charabanc outing to Weston-Super-Mare no one would ever again dare to describe that particular brand of old-time proletarian gallivanting. It has been done for good and all. There is a universal quality about the Gloucestershire excursion which the poet has captured and enshrined for ever. I implore my readers to turn up the wonderful therapeutic chapter in *Cider with Rosie* and laugh again at and with those rare human beings.

I must say something of Sunday School itself. I fear its quality did not deserve celebration in a yearly anniversary. It was always noisy and disorderly and ate up the nervous strength and patience of several good people who victimised by habit allowed their good nature and sense of duty to drive them to Sunday School every week.

Mr Prynn was the superintendent, Mr Way his deputy, and Nellie Rowse the mild efficient long-suffering secretary who stood throughout the proceedings at a lectern at the side of the room. I can't remember that silence was ever achieved though it was constantly being called for.

We started with a hymn and prayer. Then the gathering split up into classes, girls and boys separate, and teachers often competed with their charges in shouting each other down. I know that Eddie and his pals always succeeded in persuading Johnny Dunn to tell them fishing yarns.

Mrs Kymbrell took our class and we went into the chapel for a bit of peace and to hear the lesson that she had always carefully prepared. She had talked patiently for about twenty minutes while a row of adolescent girls chatted amongst themselves: I used to feel so sorry for her, conscientious and inoffensive as she was. The strain of trying to oblige her by listening and not seeming to be a prig was quite considerable. Too much of course was expected of children in those days: they were lectured and suppressed all the week in state institutions and then expected to defer to their elders again on Sunday afternoons irrespective of the weather.

At the age of twelve I became a Sunday School teacher myself, and was put in charge of the infants who sat on small chairs with round backs inside two ample red velvet curtains at the vestry end of the schoolroom. Often the boys would disappear in the folds of the curtains and roll about, the velvet covering the whole of their bodies except heads and feet. Insolent eyes peered out from the apertures, and feet tap-danced on the bare boards. For six years I bore with these infants: perhaps I grew to like them? At eighteen I remember telling Mr Prynn that I was going to Bristol University and must leave my infant class. He could not conceal his incredulity and dismay and I saw the fright behind his eyes while thoughts about a possible successor raced through his mind.

It is strange, is it not, that most of us playing different roles carry about with us private and important worlds no hint of which we convey to many of those whom we regularly meet.

For six years my most important world had been St Austell County school but in the context of Mevagissey Sunday School, the former was submerged and posed no threat to the latter.

Father too had a class tucked away in a corner under the window, and at Christmas he used to buy each of his boys a book. I imagine Mother regarded this as a foolish piece of altruism but she grew tolerant developing a 'That's how it is with your father' attitude. 'You won't change him.'

During the last prayer Marjorie tells me her row of girls exchanged information about what sort of tinned fruit they'd be having for tea. I daresay the tin and the variety were often both invented. The final prayer always included a plea to God that we should all meet an unbroken family around his throne of grace ('Stop that row, I say') Amen.

We broke up. It was still only three o'clock. I used to go home with Ruth Way, and watch her stand on a chair in the kitchen, remove a tin from the top of the dresser, lower herself down to ground level again, and take out a sweet cake. She replaced the tin, and ate the cake. No adults about! She was never discovered. We walked then perhaps to Cheese Warne or Lane End.

In the summer of 1970, returning to Mevagissey, I picked my way amongst the rubble where our Wesleyan Chapel had stood. It had been razed to the ground. The hot sun beat relentlessly down on a great aching gap in the heart of the village and on my head full of aching dismay. Who had conceived of this savage act of sacrilege, who executed this wanton piece of destruction?

All round were dwellings the fronts, sides, or backs of which had not before been exposed to the public gaze, habitations sheltered until now by a beneficient mass of masonry. Perched on high Cap'n's white house and above that Dr Grier's crenellated ivy-covered 'castle' looked perilously near to falling into the cavity below, as if they too must follow a friend into oblivion.

I had not entered the chapel for forty-eight years, but now it rose up before me entire: the stones began speaking, solemn, music filled my ears. My heart was enacting its own requiem for the dead, for past time, for the spirit of man, working man, crushed and rising again. Amongst the ruins I looked for the ashes of the phoenix which resurrected would soar up and up into the blue Cornish heaven.

Since 1970 a block of faceless flats has been erected where our chapel stood. I wonder if the occupants ever hear the singing, if they know how near they are to the green pastures and the still waters where Mevagissey fishermen and their families found shelter from those storms which raged sometimes without, and sometimes within.

Our chapel should have remained and become a new community centre with a library, a theatre, a museum, a rest room for the old, a gathering place for the young, and for those visitors who love Cornwall and all that is left of our beautiful village. Alas! these are not the notions of property developers, nor of those who in the name of progress pursue false gods, trampling on the past and its treasures with heavy undiscriminating tread.

V

17 Tregoney Hill

This was our new abode into which we moved when I was eight. It is the tall granite building just below the first sharp bend of the hill which has since been given the grand name of Buckingham House, and where summer visitors now disport themselves.

In the fabric of that house there surely must still be some residuum of the intense joy, the gaiety and dedication that went into our preparation and occupation. It was yet another occasion for the singing of the Doxology, the co-opting of the heavenly host to assist us in our thanks.

Ah yes, it was fantasy realised, a dream come true, our going to No 17. From the start our Edith had promised us something like this, without ever believing in the possibility of it herself. Faithfully she had taken us into regions of the imagination where we should want for nothing. When she died at seventy-four in 1971 she still looked very young. It was a capacity of hers to escape into dreamland, to reject the imperfect, to claim eternal life, fabricating it from chains of words which she wove into a reality more real than everyday life. What I loved best of all was the little decorated brass bell-pull which sprang out as if on elastic. It was always kept shining, and the granite stone scrubbed white. We had a garden and an attic, and a well in the back yard, a mahogany rail to the spiral staircase and a coloured glass door to the lavatory half way up the first flight. Besides which there was a creeper over the kitchen wall, and smooth blue stone steps down to the wooden garden door in the high wall of the hillside.

Oh the joy of it, the delight, the glory, the incredibility! It didn't matter that we had to wait for furniture. How we ran up and down and in and out, and laughed and argued, and planned, and pored-over patterns.

I can hear Mother singing as she worked and the rumble of cart-wheels on the hill. I can smell tar and new bread, lilies of the valley, apples, spice cake, roast pilchards and mansion polish.

The house has I believe suffered surgery within, and obviously without, where modern windows have eaten up the top part of the eastern wall. In our time one small eye, looked out to sea from that granite expanse. It was the side window of the boys' bedroom and had a smooth window seat. Mother took up her position there when the *Ibis* was out in bad weather. I have seen her remain in that window for what seemed hours, just like a statue, oblivious of everything, the muscles of her face taut, her eyes full of an intense life. It was her task to watch, and she went right out of herself, riding the storms with terrific concentration in order to bring her menfolk, four of them, safely home. What will-power, what devotion, and she, so slight and volatile.

That corner window was also the watch-tower of the cat. The eleventh member of our family, she was a silken-haired tortoiseshell with an enigmatic face and handsome tail. She sat there, serene, composed, proprietorially, smugly confident and as still as a china cat, until that moment when her eye caught the figure of the first of the boys to appear at the bottom of the hill. The air became electric: she streaked down two flights of stairs, raced through the back kitchen to the garden, and with tail in the air, paraded on the edge of the high wall to greet her family.

There was fish for her of course, supplied almost immediately, but I am sure that cupboard love was laced with a subtler regard, elicited by the step of that brother who never forgot her, his voice, his smile, the affectionate patting of her head, all of which she acknowledged by flourishes of the tail and peculiar cries. The fish could wait until greetings were exchanged, the little courtesies of life observed.

These homecomings were always exciting. Where had they been? What of the weather, and what of the catch? Sometimes they were too tired to speak, their eyes blood-shot with weariness in their weather-beaten faces. There were four of

Left to right: Myself at two years, Dick (12)
Mr Bice and Dollie

Granfer Pollard.
He always squared his shoulders

Off to the Blackhead for a picnic in the *Ibis*.
Quays empty of 'strangers'.

Archie at sixteen years.
Jules Toullec's presentation

Edith at twenty-four years.
About to say something funny.

17 Tregoney Hill.
A sketch by Peter Markey.

them to remove sea-boots, oilskins, sou'westers and thin overalls, four of them to wash and be fed. Mother was always prepared. Life was full of drama, of departures and arrivals, of exits and entrances, of large meals round a crowded table, of noises in the early mornings when tides demanded a start at dawn, of long silences during the days when they slept before leaving at nightfall, 'Be quiet now, the boys are in bed.'

Our house was the larger part of a block which contained one other dwelling having fewer rooms and no garden. When we went to No 17, this was occupied by Mr Peters the policeman, his wife Ethel and their Airedale dog. Mr Peters was a handsome man, dark, dignified, well-spoken, his sobriety tempered by a charming smile and sparkling eye. Ethel made a model housewife, her white starched apron always spotless and her shining fair hair falling perfectly round her neat face. I got the idea that the lineaments of that face were cast by concentration on cooking. Shrewdness and good temper made way for each other in her nature. She used to complain a bit about money, but as our Mother, ignorant of their actual situation, but ready to speculate, said, not to Mrs Peters but to us, 'You're bound to be hard-up if you decide always to save a fixed amount before you start spending.' Then she gave one of her embarrassed little chuckles, concealing a sense of guilt that she wasn't such a paragon herself.

There was a small room at the side of the Peters's house where sometimes a 'prisoner' would be incarcerated overnight. This filled me with horror. I never wanted to know about it: that the Law and Punishment should come so near to us was inconceivable. I imagined the 'subject' would be kept on bread and water and couldn't understand how Mrs Peters seemed so unaffected by it all.

There were no children in that house then, and Marj and I were invited next door almost every day. Mr Peters would seat us at the big table in the kitchen and take out paper and pens. I remember once his cautioning me in a solemn voice not to write too fast.

Marj and I slept together in the top back bedroom and almost always sang ourselves to sleep, Marj taking the treble and I the alto. Our favourite song was Larboard Watch Ahoy.

> At dreary midnight's cheerless hour
> Deserted e'en by Cynthia's beam
> When tempest beat and torrents roar
> And twinkling stars no longer gleam
> > No longer gleam
> The weary sailor spent with toil
> Clings firmly to the weathered shroud,
> Sings as he views the gathering cloud,
> > Larboard watch ahoy,
> > Larboard watch ahoy.

Down in the courtyard below Mr Peters would be standing listening and when we had finished he clapped loudly and cried, 'Encore Encore.' By this time the moon had perhaps risen. Ah yes of course that was Cynthia! Good old moon come to say goodnight to us.

We were so safe, surrounded by so many friends, so much affection, we were able to support the poor sailors in danger, and sang our hearts out in sympathy. Happily we fell asleep.

Father and Mr Peters became friends, and worked together to keep their fellow creatures clear of the law. They had an arrangement that Mr Peters should remain out of sight when the pubs closed, and give Father a chance to get anyone drunk and disorderly home by means of persuasion and physical support if necessary.

Mr Peters said of Father that he was 'the least gullible of men.' And yet he loved ideas of equality, of the dignity of man, of the responsibility of each for all, and there was no curing him of trust though he often looked very sad. Mr Peters I imagine had a personal God, but I doubt if Father was so buttressed, and the going was probably much harder for him than for his tall young friend.

Mr Peters got promotion, but not for the number of his arrests, and was posted to Saltash. Marjorie and I were invited there to stay and went on our first train journey ever, in charge of the guard. What a splendid institution is a guard with a green flag. I should like one to be present when I die, but Marj says I may only deserve the flag to be red.

Mr Peters was on the platform to greet us smiling and eager, and at the top of the hill stood Mrs Peters neat and beautiful as ever. Later on they had the son they so much wanted, and Mr Peters became an Inspector of Police. When Marj was training as a nurse in the South Devon Hospital, he was one of her patients, and they were photographed together.

Below us lived Cap'n and Mrs Chesterfield and their family Henry, Charlie, Annie and Lizzie, all of whom were then grown up and working away, but they were at home frequently. Lizzie is alive still, and we visit her in Truro.

It was a charming house with a climbing pink geranium on the wall, and moss roses in the square of garden inside the green railings. Mrs Chesterfield, such a lady, had a quiet gracious way of opening her door to you, and inside all was shining, tasteful and orderly. Cap'n Charlie who died when he was sixty, was often away at sea. We liked it when he came home, genial and unpretentious as all the Chesterfields were. Edith was a friend of Annie, a teacher, and Lizzie, a post office clerk, and was always exchanging books with them, and entertaining the household with acting and mimicry. Lizzie used to read aloud to her mother while she sewed, but left out the love scenes which Mrs Chesterfield said wasn't fair.

Opposite us was the one-storeyed dwelling with a narrow front courtyard enclosed by a low wall where lived Mr and Mrs Opie, Abram and Charlotte. Abram was very tall, shy and well-spoken, a man of few words. Charlotte with a deep voice, and as deep a fund of good nature took on the task, easy for her, of communication.

She was an early riser, and having finished her work before the sun was up, went down to help her sister Tilly Warren in the greengrocer's shop. Dick used to call Mr Opie, Charlotte Opie's, Abram linking him with Charlotte Bronte's Professor.

As time went on we acquired various pieces of furniture, and it was a great day when Criddle and Smith's delivered an Axminster carpet in dark blue and pink for the upstairs sitting room. The suite that went with it is still in use. We had a pair of large pictures illustrating the story of Ruth and Naomi.

In one Naomi was taking leave of her widowed daughter-in-

law, but Ruth pleaded to be allowed to go with her to the
strange land. In the second the handsome Boase was making
Ruth welcome in the fields. I used to read those words over
and over 'Entreat me not to leave thee, for whither thou goest I
will go, and where thou lodgest I will lodge, thy people shall
be my people, and thy God my God.'

Father went to a sale at St Ewe Rectory where he bid for
and had a very heavy piano knocked down to him. Just how
that piano got up the spiral staircase will never be known. It
got stuck by the coloured glass door of the lavatory. A small
army of fishermen, superintended by Stanley Behennah
executed the operation 'Steady boys. Now then. Heave Ho'.
Mother's face down below was pinched with terror and she
lapsed into hysterical laughter when the instrument as she
called it, reached the landing.

One of the pieces of furniture to grace our dining room was
a red mahogany desk which Father had had made. It was a
monstrosity, but as precious to him as the Ark of the Lord to
the Israelites. You couldn't sit at it because the head of the
couch didn't leave room. Father loved his pens and papers,
and he used to order ropes from Bridport for the *Ibis*, and for
anyone else who wanted them, but not as a business venture.

Then there were letters to the administrators of the Lascar
Fund. Lascars were East Indiamen employed in the British
Merchant Service whose lives were insured. If they died before
the Insurance became due, deposits went into a Lascar Fund
for poor sailors, and a small pension of 5/– a week could be
granted to anyone poor enough to qualify, and with the
enterprise to make application. It was Father's pleasure to
write letters for those who badly needed that 5/– and he never
failed to procure it.

Then one of Julyan's men called with pictures of settees,
and Mother succumbed to his blandishments. She decided to
get rid of the couch, and go in for a mock-leather settee in
brown with velvet cushions. What a sad day when Father
came home and found his couch gone. It was like the end of
the world. He didn't get angry, but he was utterly grief-
stricken, which was worse. Poor Mother. It didn't make
matters any better that she missed the couch too (although

she never lay on it) and secretly disliked the brown intruder from Julyan's. However time heals, and we learn to live with our mistakes.

We painted the attic blue and white. If you put your head far enough out of the window, you seemed to be suspended in space, able to drop at will into the top of an elm tree, or on to the lighthouse. I repaired to the warm remoteness of the attic very often, in order to read, and so that I shouldn't be able to hear if I were called. When we had visitors, Marj and I slept there, and the bed had a patchwork quilt of small bright silk squares. Those patterns and colours have never left my brain; they set the mind working in a thousand different directions, all pleasant.

It was a nasty shock to us all, when one day, Mother caved in. The collapse of herself didn't enter into her scheme of things, and consequently not into ours. Necessity dictated immunity, as it has done for so many of our undemanding indefatigable mothers. Marj came home from school to find her in a sorry state huddled in the big chair, alone in the house. Luckily Mr Peters was off duty: he carried her in his arms up two flights of stairs. She was a light burden which he bore tenderly. Sensing danger he got the doctor and Mother lived to be eighty-four.

We hadn't been very long at No 17, when Dr Sam Hunkin, brother of Eddie and Wilber, came home from America whither he had emigrated, and where he had gained a fine reputation as a skilful surgeon. Anxious to do what he could for his native village he opened a surgery for consultation purposes and Mother took Dollie to see him. Dollie had a congenital dislocated hip, which no one locally knew how to treat, and which in adolescence began increasingly to trouble her. Dr Sam was acquainted with a surgeon, a Mr Trethowan, and a Cornishman, who he thought might possibly undertake to operate on the leg, and he very kindly got in touch with him.

The upshot of the matter was that Dollie went to Guy's Hospital where she stayed for more than six months, and had two severe operations.

When, many years later she had occasion to enter hospital

for some minor matter, medical men were greatly intrigued by
the marks of that early surgery which had ensured that she
was kept successfully on her feet throughout her life.

It was very exciting when Dollie came home from London
on her crutches. Marj was in bed with measles, and before
anyone knew, away up the stairs on those crutches went
Dollie, not even waiting for food and drink, before seeing
Marj. It wasn't so very long before she was in the sea again
and swimming. The salt water had always been kind to her
legs and in that element she surpassed those who were whole.

Marj ailed and complained of vague pains. She lay in bed in
the top back bedroom, still smiling, but apathetic. Dr Walker,
serious, earnest, clever and middle-aged was unable to
decide what was the matter with her. He and Mother stood
together at the bottom of the bed, and the conversation ran as
follows:

Dr W: I suppose, Mrs Lakeman, she doesn't happen to have
         had any worms.
Mother: No, doctor, no.
Marj: Oh yes, I have.
Dr W: Really. Tell me about it.
Marj: I got out of bed, doctor, to use the po, and found a
         worm coming out of the back of me.
Dr W: What did you do with it?
Marj: I threw it out of the window.
Dr W: Why?
Marj: Because I didn't like it; it was nasty.

Dr Walker smiled, kindly and understanding as he was, and
interested in us all as individuals. He prescribed the powder
necessary to .get rid of the roundworm and Marj was soon
herself again, no longer a host to the parasite which had
disgusted her so much that she had needed to keep it to herself.

There were epidemics of a particularly virulent influenza
which overtook us at intervals. I fell victim to it myself, and
remember waking from a troubled sleep in the early hours of
the morning to find Father sitting anxiously vigilant at my
bedside.

'Father', I said, 'I would like to die.'

'No, no, my tar,' he said, 'no, no, not yet.'

He took my hand and willed me better.

When he himself was dying of cancer, every one of us in turn sat by his bedside, yearning over him. To ease the pain of parting I needed to write.

The light is fading in the summer sky,
While life is ebbing in his dying frame,
And all he thought, and all he was
Entrapped in eyes on fire with death's dark flame.
Compassion floods my heart,
The tides of grief engulf my soul,
While love long stored in life's unconscious deeps
Is spent in this farewell
A conscious whole.

We had electricity early in Mevagissey. The streets were lit in 1896, the first in the country, but for water we were less well provided. The town pump, our common source of life, supplied drinking water for almost everyone, and it was fetched in earthenware pitchers, or galvanised cans. The rule for us was that whoever entered the kitchen to see an empty receptacle inside the door, went out again, down the hill and through the Mill opening to fill it up. A rough sort of justice it worked pretty well, and was one factor in the learning of submission to the inevitable.

True, there are times when encounters with empty cans make up the biggest part of experience. Besides which when full, they have a way of slopping over your feet with a nasty little smack like spring tides on windy days. It will do me good to confess that, staggering along the town bridge, I was weak enough to dread meeting any of the very grand older girls from St Austell County down to spend an hour or so in quaint Mevagissey.

For washing water, soft, we had a big tank with a tap in the back court and a right of way to a well next door when we drew water for flushing the back lavatory. That was a warm clean comfortable place with a smooth white wooden seat. You held a string to keep the door shut and coughed as a warning if you heard anyone coming.

We had a new tank built to provide water for the inside

lavatory with the coloured glass door, and Mr Jimmy Holman came to do the plumbing and attendant modernising. When the chain was pulled and the flush functioned for the first time he cried, 'There you are, Mrs Lakeman – she's a lovely thing.'

While he was operating Jimmy fell into the tank, when it was full of water, after which a wide plank was laid across for his convenience. Father, concerned for his safety, called to him and he answered very respectfully, 'It's all right, sir, I'm on the plank.' This phrase we used for ever more to convey security, well being, success. I remembered it, and I must admit, with tears when in Emily Dickinson, again, I discovered this verse.

I stepped from plank to plank,
A slow and cautious way,
The stars about my head I felt,
About my feet, the sea.

I knew not but the next
Would be my final inch,
This gave me that precarious gait
Some call experience.

It could so well be a fisherman's verse, and how my father and his shipmates would have loved it. The stars were for ever about their heads, shining in the lofty summer heavens, and as brightly as in the great spaces of the mind, when during black nights of bitter storm, they were for a while obscured. I remember when we visited the Peters's at Saltash being asked to sing to some visitors, and gave a tremulous rendering of

Twinkle, twinkle little star,
How I wonder what you are,
Up above the world so high
Like a diamond in the sky.

Billie Barron who succeeded the policeman as our neighbour had a tank built soon after the construction of ours. It was so small that Dick christened it 'The Mighty Atom', that scientific phenomenon which was entering our lives just then, and being split. There could hardly have been enough water in Billie's tank to allow of the baptism of an infant.

Another phrase too appeared about that time, 'within the framework of the Locarno Pact'. It served to describe delimiting factors of all kinds.

We rarely had fires in Mevagissey, but there was a fierce one which broke out in Mr Willie Furse's garage in what must have been the late summer of 1923. The garage was at the base of Willie's house just round the sharp bend of the hill, and was let to Willie Barron to accommodate one of the very few cars then owned in the village.

The fire broke out soon after midnight and threatened to become a mighty conflagration and burn us all down. A great cloud of sparks rained past our bedroom window into the back court as I removed my gymslip hanging in the cupboard, and rushed out into the garden with it on a hanger. It was my new school uniform for St Austell County School, and more important to me then than any other possession. I encountered Mother on the stairs carrying a deed-box, and saw the back of Father, his braces dangling, disappearing through the front door shouting FIRE FIRE. Next day he hadn't any voice.

Johnny Libby's house stood next to the garage, and he emerged, hugging his deed-box and asking for someone to take it down the hill to Mrs Chesterfield's. It would be safe there in more ways than one. Eddie, unrecognised in the hubbub, was first asked his name before being entrusted with the transit of the box. Half the village left their beds, and every tank was emptied before the St Austell Fire Brigade had belatedly rattled down the moors to extinguish what still remained of the fire. Our houses all stood intact. I hung up my gymslip again, and sighed with satisfaction.

Eddie tells of another fire when Willie Whitford raised the alarm in the front street. He came out holding up his flannel drawers, the sort that had a blue horizontal stripe at intervals, and matched his cries of FIRE to the rhythms and tempo of his running. As the first impetus of his performance declined, so his cries got feebler, allegro gave way to andante, and FIRE became FIGH—YER, finally breaking on to the illuminated air as the ghost of a sigh. It was a 'Greater love hath no man than this' effort, a complete abandonment of self to the good of the community. Every year or two afterwards Eddie would re-enact it for us, so that the event was revived to remain green in our minds. 'Remember,' Eddie would say, 'Willie was running *away* from the fire.'

Soon after the fire came the wreck of the French trawler on Chapel Point. The lifeboat coxswain was Mr Dennis Maher, Peggy's father, of Irish extraction and known as Dinny Me'ar. Dinny was drawn to lifeboats and life-saving by his love of drama, his vivid imagination opposing all that threatened to reduce the exciting potential of life. He abhorred whatever was monotonous, pedestrian, trivial, ordinary or dull, and did not intend that everyday things should rob existence of its essential glory. We trusted to Dinny to supply us with everything that was outsize.

Percy Hunkin, a fearless and splendid navigator, was there. All was well. We had strong feelings of fraternity with France left over from the bloody struggle with Germany not long since terminated. Cornwall was swallowed up in a larger piece of geography when Dinny, arms outstretched cried, *'I am England. Can I ——render you —— any assistance? Make way, boys, she's a monster:'* Percy saw to it that the assistance was practical. There was no loss of life and our allies were handsomely treated. Wherever should we be without a bit of swagger from somebody? Dear old Dinny, he earned our affection and returned it.

In the early twenties Granfer Lakeman came to live with us; Aunt Louie was dying and could no longer look after him.

Granfer's bed was installed in the 'big room', our upstairs sitting-room which had two long windows looking on to the hill whence he could see the world go by. A coal fire burned in the grate. Granfer would send Marj out for Pollies and they sat one each side of the fire throwing their apple cores into the flame.

Granfer was a master of hyperbole, and Gramma and Father were always afraid he would depart from the truth in more than a poetical sense. Given to understatements themselves, they were offended by 'raming,' but Mother would say, 'I don't see anything wrong with Math. He's entertaining, and has always been good to me.' He was an intelligent, if not over assiduous gardener and had an allotment in the field below the School House. I remember looking over the hedge as I came home from school, fascinated by the long straight rows, the carrot tops, the curly greens, the coral bean flowers, and the pods heavy with peas.

Granfer grew gooseberries of a size that made 'three only to the pint,' and there was a mythical cabbage that was too big to be got through the Town Hall door for a Show. From miles out to sea he swore he could see the domestics at Heligan House shaking their dusters out of the window.

He was chatty but never silly, full always of interesting bits of communication, and going down Church Street would lean over the half-doors and have a yarn with anyone, especially the women. Loft-work could wait, and in any case Richard was getting on with it. He would smack his chest and say, 'Tis all in here, but I can't get it out.' All the same he did get out quite a lot, and certainly too much for Father!

His love of natural history was genuine; he watched the clouds and the stars, he knew every tree, and the names and haunts of all the birds. I imagine he was built to enjoy himself far more than the crippling economics and inflexible moral code of our little society ever permitted. His brother and sister Ferdinand and Elisabeth, both single, lived together in a very tastefully furnished home where they had leather-bound books! Granfer had once known better times, and there was a certain bravado about him that was amusing and lovable. Edith inherited his fine nose and fertile imagination.

He enjoyed his food which one or the other of us took up to him. He used to rap on the floor with his stick when hunger assailed him. It never failed to surprise me how patient Mother was. 'Hurry up now,' she would say, 'one day you'll be old yourself and will know how it feels.' He always had bread and milk with salt and pepper before going to bed. Father bathed him on Sunday mornings before chapel-time. He was tall and lean and had very white skin. He died as befitted him, detached and without anguish, was just poorly for a few days, and departed. When Emma Sears laid him out, she said he made 'a handsome corpse' and taking Marj by the hand led her in to see him, 'Come on my dear,' she said, 'come in and see how lovely your granfer looks.' It was an easy natural approach to death. The fourth of our grandparents was gone.

Up the hill, on the bend, facing downwards was a small chapel known as Reform, founded by a splinter group of Methodists. First the Bible Christians, nick-named Prickly Backs, broke away from the Wesleyans, and then the Reformers dissented from the Prickly Backs.

I haven't any knowledge of the doctrinal differences, but have been reminded that the Reformers were 'kid-glove people', a small band of the socially élite which included Mr Matthias Dunn (Howard's brother) and Mrs Polly Barbary née Pearce. Polly was fascinating, neat, petite, and elegantly clad. I have some recollection of feather boas and top hats. Mother used to peer out from behind the curtain, consumed with curiosity and slightly envious to check up on current fashions.

The football ground was approached via Tregoney Hill too, and a jolly crowd passed up and down on Saturday afternoons. It seems that at one time Mevagissey Team was quite famous. The happy noise of fans, shouting and laughing as well able then to take defeat as to revel in victory, burst upon your ears. Afterwards you learned what silence was, and a particular almost palpable Saturday evening stillness fell as it were from the calendar of the skies.

The week was almost over. Time like an ever rolling stream bears all its sons (including footballers) away.

Later in the evening Town Bridge became alive again. The boys stood about in knots outside Tilly Warren's, and the girls minced up and down in their Saturday evening clothes (different from Sunday best.) There was assessment of legs from the bystanders. Marj tells me how she loved to slip away and go down there for just a few minutes. However tragic the times, even as now, there is always a great army of young ones hopefully setting out on life in expectation of joy. Towards ten o'clock Bessie Lobb went up the hill in her cart, home to Kestle. She was a big woman, and wore an old wide-brimmed felt hat and dark coat, and drove her horse and cart in the style of Boadicea. One Saturday evening, when it was getting 'dimsy' and as the horse changed gear in the steep part of the hill outside our garden door, the silence was shattered by a resounding two-syllabled cry. Bessie's passenger must at that crucial moment have imparted to her the incredible, in answer to which she gave a great bleating reply of *'Never.'* It burst on the night air with a force that no denial can ever have exceeded, and we *never* forgot it. How we longed to know what it was that Bessie could scarcely believe!

Granfer Lobb used to walk home to Kestle carrying a stout stick, and put it to uses other than mere support. Margaret Robins came in to Mother one day.

'You know Mrs Lakeman,' she said 'there iden a stingeen nettle left on the right 'and 'edge between 'ere and Kestle.'

'Oh Margaret, how is that?'

'How? Wey, Granfer Lobb, and that stick of his.'

Occasionally we had the odd singer, begging. He would probably come from the Clay District where in the twenties unemployment was rife. This one dragged his leg, and gazing heavenwards sang 'Guide me Oh Thou Great Jehovah.' 'Oh dear, there he is again. Poor ole Guide-me-Oh. Where's my purse?'

A regular visitor to our house was Stanley. Combining in himself every fascinating feature of the Behennahs, he was tall and broad, grand in his movements, his gestures, his ideas, and his outlook in general. Nothing limited or stuffy about Stanley. His figure resembled Aneurin Bevan's, and like Aneurin, he was afflicted at one time with a slight stammer. For a while he went on the *Ibis* with Father, and they did deep-breathing and elocution exercises upon the bow as a cure. Stanley improved.

Stanley slipped in to see Mother often, for he lived just around the corner, he and Adelaide, his beautiful wife. He entertained Mother with current gossip which Father never heard, nor would have repeated if he had. Stanley could act any part so that material was dramatised and splendidly produced. What need had Mother to travel to St Austell to see plays? What more appreciative audience could Stanley have wished for than Mrs Lakeman? Who quicker to laugh? Who readier to cry? They each had that streak of melancholy which accompanies a strong sense of humour, and the same hysteria afflicted them when events took the preposterous turn they so often have a way of doing. In any case when two such people as Mother and Stanley got together, all the world came to look ridiculous, and in what was then their 'theatre of the absurd' they laughed until they cried.

Mr Floyd, a local preacher who was a pack-man on weekdays came at intervals. His goods were surrounded by a waterproof cover, held together by two straps. The pack was opened up on the kitchen floor in front of the Cornish range, and revealed every kind of drapery, wrap-over aprons, towels, ticking, dusters, lace, pillowcases, runners, and remnants, and always a particular 'Good line.' Mother was intrigued by that pack, consumed with interest, aching to spend. It was manna from heaven for the hungry. Mr Floyd was so mild, so obliging, so ready to turn everything over, and to unroll it, to hang it up, and never pushing of his wares. He knew Mother would buy, and she always did. Sometimes though when he came to the 'good line', she would remember Dick making a joke of it, and have to disappear into the other room ostensibly to get her purse, but actually to gain control of herself.

Mr Harry Tregaskis used to come every week from Galowras Farm, carrying a huge basket of butter, round shaped, and stamped with the benignant head of a cow. Galowras Farm is in the region of Scotland Woods where anemones star the slopes in early spring, and irises unfurl their purple and yellow flags in the gluey marshes. Up on the skyline Gorran Church rules the landscape like an island lighthouse, and illuminated by the moon speaks of glory and blessedness in worlds unknown. I never knew Ann Treneer, but I would love to have spoken to her about it. She attended that church.

Mr Tregaskis was a good-looking man. I believe he wore shiny leather gaiters, and a tweed sports coat and cap. The width of his basket reduced his height but in any case he was no Piers Plowman.

A stranger to optimism, not even over vast areas of good fortunes could he have arrived anywhere near hopefulness. He was solemnly friendly, humble and unassuming, and now I think of it, Mother must have raised his spirits by making the manifold difficulties of life and particularly his, her chief subject of conversation. What is more she didn't forget a word of praise for the excellent produce which came out of his basket. Then faces were serious while the kitchen filled up with goodwill, and before he left Mr Tregaskis was almost happy, smiling his slow uncertain smile. Later on he had bright children, and life took on new dimensions for him.

The Adamses, two or three brothers came from Treninick Farm on the Gorran Road. They arrived on a Saturday night with bags of potatoes, and would sit sometimes for as long as an hour on upright chairs on the dining room before going down the hill for a taste of life on the Town Bridge. The land produced a species of worker quite different from us who lived by and on the sea. They were more stolid than we, who had always to be striving to keep a balance, and could only achieve it even so with a slightly rocking gait.

Cap'n Pollard (Edwin), Mother's first cousin, son of Jack, visited us every week with his wife Emmie. Emmie, a younger woman hailed from Kent, and the middle class, and fell in love with Cap'n when she met him on a voyage. Cap'n had a fine house build further up the hill Pen-Pol, which testifies still to the excellent workmanship of Mr Willie Pearce, master-builder, a native, and a Wesleyan.

Cap'n made a paradise of the garden, and his industry acting on the fertile soil, with her efficiency allied to middle-class comforts indoors, produced an establishment which gave us our first and startling introduction to high living.

Turkey carpet, silver trays, a dresser of huge proportions surpassing Edith's fictitious article, a pianola which played 'Land of Hope and Glory' (Conservatism was rife) bottled fruits in real screw-top jars, fresh strawberries unrationed, palm trees which bore flowers, apples that over-flowed all containers, pears that ripened as you watched, solid, tasty, seedless tomatoes, and luscious grapes in tight bunches enlarged and enriched our conception of life.

Cap'n (Edwin) drove a car through the streets, then obligingly empty of other traffic, and Emmie in her amber beads wore a picture hat the like of which had never before been seen in Mevagissey. Earrings dangled to the slow motion of the car. Watchful eyes, described by Ann Treneer in *School House in the Wind* took everything in without giving the slightest sign of being impressed.

On Saturday evenings the two of them would come into No 17 and if Marjorie and I had gone to bed, we'd be called down again. We appeared in our home-made nightgowns, dressing-gowns not then constituting part of working-class children's wardrobes. Marj sat on Cap'n's knee, while I curled up in front of the fire delighted as always with adult company, and the pictures that appeared in the glowing coals.

Cap'n was tanned and sparkling. His thin grey hair curled round a beaming face, and he was charmingly natural and especially good with children. Alas he hadn't any of his own.

Cap'n wore pale grey very fine well-tailored suits, and in summer, Panama Straw Hats. He carried a gold-topped cane matched by a gold tooth. Mrs always had a photograph of him on her table and he superseded all upper-class connections in her regard. Mrs's tall very ample body was carried on thin shapely legs and her delight in her husband she transferred to any of his relatives who chose to accept her. She it was who 'decided' that Marj must positively take up nursing.

She had a powerful presence, which often sent me to sleep, worn out by the force of her personality. Much older than his wife, Cap'n died long before she did, and when she was near her own end she talked always of Edwin, of the old days in Mevagissey, of the trustworthiness of everyone, of the laughter and the love, and of Mary Sarah, 'your dear mother'. Father she never mentioned, and neither did I, although, had she but known, he was the one to see her side of things (as far as he could) and to point out how difficult she must have found it, adapting to village life in Cornwall.

I think she and Cap'n were uneasily aware of areas of experience he never attempted to share with them, that he lived on territory which did not appear upon the map of life they had so confidently drawn for themselves. He never failed to be courteous and kind.

Mrs learnt her husband's brand of generosity and happy in

his protection, she certainly mellowed with the years. One interesting thing I found about her and her only, and it applied even when she was old and lonely and ill, she had the capacity of making me feel for a short while that I was in a safer world, solid, material, uncomplicated, shut off from the dangers of introversion, without qualms of conscience, of painful self-doubt. From contact with her I learned about the great differences in temperaments and mental geography, and I learned in a practical way about the necessity of tolerance. I believe that at one time she eyed me suspiciously, sensing dangerous unorthodoxy, adamantine convictions, revolutionary radicalism, but in time she tolerated me too, and smiled with loving gratitude when I made her the salads she ate with such relish.

Wesleyan Ministers called on us, but the only one to become a close friend was the Reverend Picken. He came always to the back door, tapped lightly and walked in. He'd sit with his elbows on the kitchen table, his strong sad face cupped in his long hands, and discuss human relationships. His frustrations and bewilderment once poured out, he became lively, even merry; and forgetting all the problems connected with the stiff-necked of his flock, he was Minister no longer, but a companion, a brother to us who helped him care less about things he would never be able to alter.

I have a friend who, within one frame has photographs of those people who have greatly influenced his life in a beneficent fashion. Were I to assemble such a collection Mr Picken would be given a prominent place.

Once I remember we entertained an elderly supernumary and his wife, and so we said grace and he was asked to 'pronounce the blessing.' Towards the end articulation failed him, and he concluded with 'For Jesus Christ's cake.' We wondered if the sight of saffron and sweet seed had affected his vocal cords. When his wife helped herself to the cream so liberally as utterly to flout egalitarian principles, we were rather shocked. Not good enough this in a Wesleyan! We learned justice through the medium of clotted cream.

There appeared in Mevagissey the first Labour Candidate for our constituency and I think his name was Shepherd. He needed to be put up for the night and there was nowhere for him to go.

'What about it, Mother?' Father asked, 'Can we manage it?'

'Well yes I should think so, if he doesn't mind a crowd,' she replied. So he came, a young man and very friendly, and seemed to enjoy himself, though of course he wasn't returned to Parliament.

At least once a month Marion was home for the weekend from Truro. She brought with her a Cathedral City, Rural, Conversative, and Post Office culture as a shot-in-the-arm to our maritime remoteness. Her basket overflowed with Truronian produce, butter, sweet biscuits and firm fat tomatoes, a recent addition to the national diet. Eddie 'fell to' on the tomatoes which he loved. City fashion was another import. Marion wore fantastic fruit and flower-laden hats. One was in the shape of a beehive, and when after morning service there was the usual walk to the end of the quay, we hung back so as not to be too closely associated with such daring headgear.

Then popular songs rang through the house, 'Mother Machree', 'Little Grey Home in the West', 'Mifanwy' and 'Because'. Marion sang while I did my juvenile best at the piano, better always at chords, especially the final one, than anything in between. Her voice was quite splendid, and being trained in Truro, rang out to advantage, much too far for Dick who sped round the house shutting all the windows.

Later on Harry, her young man, was brought home and Edith, on holiday, became anxious about drinks. 'We must have tea, coffee, *and* cocoa in the house, Mother,' she said. A rehearsal was staged. 'What will you have, Father?' she asked, 'Tea, coffee or cocoa?'

Gazing into the distance, innocent and unheeding he replied, 'A cup of milk will do me.'

Harry came and was so happy he gave Marj and me half-a-crown each, a monstrous amount which completely stunned me. I suggested to Marj that we return the coin for something smaller. 'Oh go on,' she said, 'don't be so silly. I want to keep mine. Forget it.'

We had regularly walked to Kestle throughout the years to visit Great Aunt Miriam (Murry), Gramma's sister and a widow. She needed daily support now, and fortunately the one-roomed dwelling opposite us, and next to Mrs Opie's fell vacant. Aunt Murry was installed, and we took meals down to her and cleaned her room. She got better and had a new black silk coat to wear to chapel on Sunday evenings. Marj used to scrub her white-topped table very vigorously, but had to be solemnly corrected by Murry when she forgot the black soapy drops underneath the edge. Aunt Murry's great security was Jacob's Crackers, and if she was without a spare in her tin, she became quite neurotic. Marj tells me that the pleasure induced by this particular biscuit still operates amongst the elderly. Life is hard without it.

Once when I was already at the County School, and Mother and Father were actually away from home, Dollie and I decided to go blackberry picking in the morning, a bold plan. We didn't get back until after 1 p.m. and Aunt Murry stood hungrily distraught in her doorway. 'I'll tell you what,' she shouted, 'it's too much education, that's what's the matter with you, Mary!' Poor old Aunt Murry. She came up with us to die, and I can see Father now standing at the door of her room, calm and faithful, a brass oil-lamp in his hand. No son could ever have been more attentive; his presence was her consolation, and he stayed by her, to the end. She was eighty-two.

I came downstairs one morning to find a tall handsome Scotsman asleep on the couch. He had been out pilchard driving in the *Ibis* and Father had brought him home in the early hours. He was one of those romantics who wanted to identify with the fishermen, and to take a fishing expedition proper. A gracious guest, charmingly grateful for our hospitality, he was delightful to Mother. Years later when he was living in Bristol he came to know through Father that I was a student at the University, and arrived at Elton House to take me to his home. It was a beautiful flat I remember and after our meal, he put on a Bach record. Sensing however that this particular genius was a stranger to me, and discovering that I was reading history, he enquired what I thought of

Jeremy Bentham, and the Utilitarians. Unfortunately
Bentham like Bach had not yet entered my ken.

I felt embarrassed and tongue-tied and silly, and searched
fruitlessly for something to say. Then Mr G. produced another
smaller cheaper-looking record and I was startled to hear the
'Song of the Prune':

> No matter how young a prune be
> It's always full of wrinkles
> We may get them on our face
> Prunes get them every place.

And so on ending up with the certainty of 'a heart of stone'.

I opened my mouth wide and roared with laughter. The last
few hours had taxed my resources to their limit. I gave an
abandoned performance of mirth which broke down all
barriers, and soon had my host and hostess shouting with
laughter as well, not so much at the prune, but at themselves
and me, in our joint and until now, unsuccessful attempts to
put each other at ease. What did it matter that J.S. Bach, and
Jeremy Bentham had failed to elicit any response? My hosts
had given me the cue for unbending.

It was getting on towards Christmas, and the end of my first
term in Bristol. Mr G. pressed the record into my hands
telling me to take it home to Mevagissey. Longing to be there, I
could already hear our Eddie singing that song. Yet I
experienced a sense of indebtedness to these good people for a
gift which my delight had seemed almost to demand. We all
had the same grounding in never accepting anything from
anybody unless we could make adequate return. The record
was a great success and Father joined in the merriment.

Mr G. left Bristol but many years later he came back to
Mevagissey with another wife, a beautiful lady who lectured
in history. He was sad to discover that Father had died, but he
and his wife came down to Falmouth to visit Marjorie and me.
They had a splendid Kerry Blue with them who walked about
our flat like another human being, and promptly obeyed the
gentle orders his master issued to him. At last I was able to
return their hospitality. In the afternoon we went on an
excursion to Kynance Cove and the conversation flowed freely

as we jumped the rocks and strode across the springy turf. Mr
G. died in middle age.

And so the twenties, that stormy, terrible, wonderful
decade, as are all decades, drew to its close and the end of our
youth.

One by one some of the older members of our family
married, and then Mother and I delivered Marj to the South
Devon Hospital to begin her training.

All unaware we were of the almost military régime to which
she was to be subjected. Yet a sad unease possessed us, as we
sat together, silent, on a seat near the Hoe. I dared not look at
Mother, who, all eyes, stared straight out to sea as she used
always to do when the boys had been overtaken by wicked
storms. 'Precious lamb,' she murmured.

17 Tregoney Hill was too large for us. The small remaining
core of our family moved to Battery Terrace, and Father's life
was not to last much longer.

October sunshine falls aslant the hill
This Sunday afternoon
No-one about.
All still.
The lingering summer and the dying day
Defying winter and the coming night
Conspire with my protracted stay
Upon this precious patch of ground
To fill the body of my mind
With blessedness.

Dusk falls.
Farewell.
I will bequeath
All earth and heaven
All time and space
To such as step upon this place
With reverence
In autumn sun
Aslant the hill
Some Sunday afternoon
No-one about.
All still.

VI

Shops and Shopkeepers

Martha Thomas, whose shop was at the bottom of Polkirt Hill next to the entrance to the meadow, and opposite the opening to the harbour, was our Saturday evening grocer. 8 p.m. was closing time. Martha was a little lady, and single, cheerful without being boisterous, practical but not fussy, and very benevolent. You stepped down from the street on to the stone floor of the shop, half of which was covered with large baskets of fruit and vegetables. On the right you faced a solid wooden counter wide out of all proportion to ground space. A door in the right hand corner, always left open, led into Martha's abode. Shelves were stocked with ample supplies of what in those days must have been largely Empire produce. I remember particularly the fat raisins, the black treacle, the spices, and large blocks of salt.

Granny Chesterfield next door made toffee for Martha to sell, and it was delicious containing all fresh butter, for the Chesterfields without any mean streaks did nothing by halves. Then Martha indulged us by laying out the Rowntrees Gums in a row so that we could choose our favourite flavourings.

Two steps on the left as you entered led up to Mrs Hunkin's, Martha's sister's, living room. She was Mary, wife of another Albert, and mother of Albert and William the marine engineer.

Martha wore her hair looped up like curtains in nineteenth century style. Mrs Hunkin, taller and plump, had fair hair which curled round her calm countenance.

After tea Marj consulted with Mother and made a list. 'Shall I add some gum-prunes tonight, Mother?' They were a high class sweet, plum coloured in the shape of a boat, with a sugary coating. Off we went, each with a basket. Marj and Martha were great pals. They threw enthusiasm and practicality into the assembling of provisions, and made of it a companionable chatty exercise. I went up the steps for a session with Mrs Hunkin and sat at her table under the window for our weekly review of events. She was a generous woman, shedding affection and amusement of a particular quality which seemed to shimmer around her ample frame like midsummer sunshine. I loved her in the same way as I loved Mrs Burt. They both wrapped you up, somebody else's child, in a blessed tolerance, a warm protective covering inside which you could grow and thrive, Marj and Martha shared the same loving understanding. They once decided to send away Typhoo Tips coupons for a copy each of *Lorna Doone*, and Marj undertook the business, enclosing two orders in one envelope. The volumes arrived, but alas, the friends found Richard Blackmore rather heavy going, and went quiet over an unfruitful result of joint enterprise. When we came to Mary and Martha in the New Testament I gave them the faces of our friends in the shop.

On the side of what is now S.W.E.B. stood the Post Office run by Mrs Roberts, a second wife and imported. She wore black clothes and shuffled.

The shining impersonality of electrical equipment in a large modern shop makes a ridiculous contrast to the original set-up. It was 'chuck-a-block' with almost everything necessary to survival, a mass of goods all contingent upon the work of Postal Communication carried on mostly behind the scenes, telegrams and things.

Marion entered the post office as a learner at fourteen, and remained four years. Between the ages of two and six I was a daily caller at this establishment, not always welcomed however by Mrs Roberts. Perched up on the counter by Miss Ada Lelean, Senior Clerk, I obediently recited nursery rhymes which the proprietress didn't consider went well with business. 'H'm, h'm, h'm, h'm we must get on.'

Counters in front and at the sides made strong barricades with only a tiny opening leading to mysterious regions for

Staff Only. These counters accommodated blocks of lard and cheese, daily papers (for collection) stationery, dried and fresh fruit, sweets, boots and shoes, towels and blankets, something in fact from every manufacturing agency in the country. On a rope above the central counter hung kettles, frying pans, saucepans and other culinary articles. Room was found also for a lending library.

Gertie Barron, Muriel Carveth and Ada Burt were Marion's fellow-learners. They dressed the windows in blankets and saucepans, served lard and boots, walked to Portmellon with telegrams, and worked hard until eight o'clock all in return for making the acquaintance of stamps and Postal Orders, and lessons in telegraphy from Miss Lelean. They had one half-day off a week, and no pay. Mrs Roberts earning their ill-concealed scorn, offered them any Turkish Delight which the mice had nibbled, and the odd orange with one of those sore spots indicating a rotten heart. A spotted orange might accompany the shilling earned on a Sunday afternoon for three hours' work necessary when a lot of fish had been landed the day before. It was a very busy office indeed.

Marion remembers a gallant American in World War I helping her unhook saucepans from the line above the counter.

The girls engaged in furtive defiance of Mrs Roberts sending each other little parcels of raisins wrapped in brown paper and tied up with used string.

Every Friday Anne Ball, another cousin of Mother's, came with Tom trat and shrimps (home made toffee in shape of a shrimp with a nut for an eye). She was under the impression that the girls should be rewarded for her Old-Age-Pension which she seemed to think had been engineered by them and not Lloyd George. Anyhow they dispensed it and got a treacly, nutty, shining smooth return. Anne knew how to make toffee, and I always knew when it was Friday!

Ada Lelean's mother used to make toffee too, and we were told please to call and collect a tinful. Ada was a cousin of ours, a Congregationalist with a firm voice. A good telegraphist and mathematician, she had high principles and lived up to them. When Mother died in the fifties the boys decided it must be a 'Men Only' funeral, since they could better bear it without us there. The little chapel was full of men, except for Ada. She had to go, and we were glad she did.

How I loved their house with alcoves in the walls full of china. So interesting it was and sunny, so comfortable and homely. Ada used to say, 'We don't bother with window-cleaning, just leave it to the *elements.*'

Ten years ago we went to visit her in hospital when she was dying, and what a wonderful reception we had from that brave woman.

Annie Williams, afterwards Mrs Rolling, was Mrs Roberts's housekeeper, and Annie made the most delicious yeast-buns using lard from the block. She was a very capable worker. Mrs Roberts discovered a great potential in the Mevagissey population which she harnessed to the efficient and profitable running of her domestic and business life. The blanket word for it is enterprise, which they say has to be motivated by private gain.

Opposite the Post-Office was Henry Roberts's shop converted now into a café. It provided books and papers, toys and baskets, stationery, pens, pencils, paints, and cutlery. Emmie Roseveare was Henry's faithful assistant, the head and shoulders of her short body appearing above the counter at all hours of the day for long years. Emmie belonged to that percentage of the population destined to do nothing but serve and oblige, but she did it in her own no nonsense style.

Once in chapel sitting behind Edith during a prayer offered by a show-off minister Emmie said in quite a loud voice, 'What a silly man that is.' It was true, and who with a better right to say so than Emmie?

As a small boy Dick longed for a pen-knife. There was a very good one in Henry Roberts's window, and Dick would go and press his nose flat against the pane and feast his eyes upon it. He gave up the idea of possessing it, for he knew what pain it would cause Mother having to refuse him the money, should she not have it.

Many years later Marj bought a pocket dictionary at Henry's to send as a birthday present to Edith who had gone to Exeter Training College. It seems Marj was determined to ensure that seats of learning weren't neglecting essentials. She put so much diligence into the tying up, that the surface was fairly gnarled with knots, and Mother didn't have the heart to include it with the laundry as she'd intended. It had to make its way to Exeter under the distinction of separate cover.

George Hunkin's drapery store with a men's department, stood next down the street. George, a big man, was lame and walked with a crutch. He was always in the doorway probably for air as well as entertainment. I once heard him pronounce the culprit in a minor accident in the street. 'Culprit,' I thought, 'whatever is that? I must go home and look it up.' George married a tall widow with two daughters and they brought a dash of something different to the shop when occasionally they called. Their elegance, beyond our reach, was something to aim at, a Diana of the Uplands unattainable, smartly casual.

We used to go to George's for boys' caps, men's drawers and best socks. George, in debonair fashion, flung whatever we chose into a large bag, and the goods were taken home on approval without any records being made of what went in. Caps passed from head to head, peaks undone and fastened again with a snap. 'Too small. Here's a 7¼. Right we'll have these three, and four pairs of drawers. Say thank-you to Mr Hunkin mind.'

It was the same with shoes. We went to Lennard's and gingerly ascended Tregoney Hill carrying a pile of boxes precariously aslant like the Tower of Pisa held between the base of trunk and uplifted chin. 'Lovely – Look. Black patent mother, with straps. Can we have a pair?'

On the corner at the bottom of Tregoney Hill where fringed suede waistcoats and lambswool hats now tempt the fashion conscious, was Tommy Thomas's shop, graced by Margaret Robins who might have made a good Ombudsman. She died young, a very capable girl.

Marj remembers placing her small hoard of savings in Margaret's hands with a plea for advice about a birthday present for Dollie, aged seventeen, imprisoned in Guy's Hospital. Now Margaret said *grapes* were the thing for anyone sick. So half-a-pound of best black were included in the multi-partite parcel and Tommy Thomas served a hospital inmate in the capital with luxury fruit.

Across the way was May Ball's, an important place which features in the story of my early years. May served cream from Tregiskey farm and we stood, elbows on counter gazing at her weighing the glass preparatory to filling it. It was an exercise in absolute justice. She used small coins, farthings and sixpenny bits in addition to weights to achieve a perfect balance before the crisp spongy layers of yellow cream were fastidiously laid in the glass, and then the two together would have to correspond to the increased weight on the other side. Time was an immaterial factor. It was my initiation into the importance of Scales, and it gave me pleasure to find them again in the outstretched hand of the Statue of Liberty. Would not May have been an asset in Washington on a few occasions?

Down from Tommy Thomas's was Granfer Williams's great dairy paved in blue stone, and housing huge pans of cream. It stretched back so far you could get lost in the half-light of cool cavernous depths. Marjorie, the grandchild, later Eddie's wife, appeared in that remote region, her black shining ringlets bobbing up and down. We felt a certain reverence for curls and pearl slides because neither had come our way.

Looking towards the Town Bridge and opposite the Ship Inn was Tilly's, Tilly Warren's, greengrocer's. The big window is now full of branch bakery. It faces you as you enter the village, and Tilly faces me, an unforgettable figure as I look back.

You entered the shop at the side, up two steps as deep as your legs were long, and there she was, always in an extra-long double breasted, well belted, dun-coloured raincoat and never without her big hat turned up at the back and down in front.

Steadfast, genuine, gruff, very nearly blind, and single, she knew you by your step and hazy outline, and standing in the space between counter and window turned sharply with a little grunt of a friendly greeting. 'A gallon of potatoes (10 lbs.) and a pottle (4 lbs.) of apples Miss Warren please.' She was always busy and would often ask you to serve yourself. The great scoop of a scale stood against the wall, and bending to pick up the weights we'd begin throwing earthy potatoes into the scoop. Tilly knew how to treat children. No effusiveness with her, just plain trust and directness.

At the back would be a small mountain perhaps of crisp savoys (I never saw a flabby cabbage in Mevagissey) and great maunds of apples stood about like pieces of furniture. Sometimes exotic fruit, bunches of bananas, would appear in the window and large platters of ripe strawberries. Auntie Etta was home with us on holiday, and we were packing a picnic in the flasket. She pressed half-a-crown into Marjorie's hand, 'Go down, my dear to Miss Warren's for a large bunch of bananas.' Marj's legs couldn't carry her down the hill fast enough. What joy! to go in to Tilly's and ask for bananas.

Tilly would feel the coin between finger and thumb determining its worth, distinguishing unerringly between florin and half-crown. The money was in a deep drawer left half open, a sea of coins, mostly pennies, which rose as the splendid kidney beans and carrots were translated into money by Tilly's good arithmetic.

She remained poor. There was a peculiar pathos about her compounded of independence, absence of self-pity and humility. Within the limits of a confined life, she was so much larger than many of society's privileged. Remembering her tall figure, I am strangely moved, and wonder about her end. Mrs Opie our Tregoney Hill neighbour, and her sister, were good to Tilly and came into the shop often to help.

Across the way in what is now Phil Cloke's restaurant Alma Robins dealt in matronly millinery, and materials. We eschewed the headgear, but purchased the textiles. Alma gave lessons to her young customers in cutting. 'Watch now, follow the point of the scissors to go straight.' She was determined to educate us which was tedious, but manners prevailed.

In a small room upstairs Edith, her musical daughter, taught us piano playing, but Alma always met us on the doorstep with the same alarming query, 'Have you practised?' I was too stupid not to say that I hadn't, and went up the stairs burdened with guilt and wishing that Alma would leave the district. Edith was gentle and patient, but her standard too high for unambitious beginners. She was a splendid performer, and I was never happier than when she acceded to my request to play the piece for me.

Next door at J.C. Rowe's the butcher's there stood a little old wooden desk, the lid of which was raised to accommodate money and bills. It was all so neat and spotless, and the fine carrot-tops under the table made a veritable grove of ferns. Mrs Rowe, a precisely spoken lady, enunciated every word with emphatic clarity. Her husband Johnny Coffin Rowe had the look of a patriarch and was interested in Egypt and the Pyramids. He gave papers wherein he wandered amongst the earliest areas of civilisation, but always came back home before he finished.

The bread and butter citadel of Town Bridge, and very heart of the village was Hicks's Baker's and Confectioner's with the great bakehouse at the back. In 1956 Kelly's Ices took over the premises, and converted what was a warm, bustling, homely, human, capacious crowded interior into a stream-lined parlour, coldly standardised like the remunerative ice-cream it produces.

Johnny Hicks started his business in a little shop well up Church Street in the nineteenth century. He and Mrs Hicks converted $17\frac{1}{2}$ lbs of flour into bread and cakes, and having sold out before evening, ventured to repeat the experiment next morning. Demand was maintained and supply kept up. Outside bakery was taken in and Mr Hicks combined jouting (hawking of fish) with his baking, taking pilchards in a cart out to the North Coast. There was one woman who when she heard his cry *'Pilchards'* put her head out of the upstairs window, shouted *'Stop'* and rushed down to fry a round of ham for Mr Hicks, a fortifier for the return journey of about twenty miles.

There were two ovens in the Church Street bakery, one large, and a smaller one behind it, and they both had floors of brick. The bottoms of the loaves had to be scraped after baking. Gladys, youngest of the Hickses, tells me that in the floods of 1903 the water rushed through the ovens and carried the dinners with it, so that they went floating down the front street past the Town Hall on the inland waves.

Johnny and his wife had a family of four boys and three girls, Tom, Charlie, Sam and Will, Ida, Carrie and Gladys.

When the boys returned from the War in 1920 the family moved to the Town Bridge House and Sam drove the first Ford, delivered to him with a few verbal instructions only. Untutored, he climbed the precipitous hills on solid tyres which took unkindly to the ice that covered road surfaces in hard winters. Some time later Tom, who travelled on a long round to Portlo and Veryan with a horse and cart, acquired a van, a huge affair, as noisy as a traction engine, which he liked much less than his horse.

Charlie always stayed in the bakehouse; Will helped him and then set off on a local round in a canvas topped cart. Will wore a long grey alpaca coat and a flat cap: he and his horse were one.

Carrie and Gladys ran the shop with Margaret (Elvins) to help them, and Tom was often in and out early, towering at the desk in the left-hand corner. Lovely crusty light wholesome bread it was, and good yeast cake, saffron and white stacked up on the right hand side. I never saw a Hicks anything but composed. They were built impassively to take the whole gamut of human behaviour from the meanest to the noblest, without failing quietly to note the significance of it all. How we loved and admired Carrie and Glad, their good looks as well as their characters.

Marj remembers going in for ¼lb. sweet biscuits for private consumption, and Glad taking down no less than three new tins, stripping off the sealing tape for her to have a really wide choice. Then, having weighed the favourites, she slipped a few raisins into the pocket of the child's pinny.

The counter was constantly being wiped down, and space cleared for orders. Somebody would come in from the back with a whispered message of great import; meaningful looks were exchanged, and eyebrows raised. Highly serious expressions dissolved into rippling laughter.

I used to love going in there on the rare occasions when it was quiet to have a little chat with Carrie. She carried her dark head slightly to one side, and a tender smile played about her mouth, which opened very wide when she laughed defeating the seriousness of her eyes. 'You reckon it up, my love, will you?'

Margaret threw herself into the business with devoted zeal, and like Peter Hocking in the bakehouse became an integral part of it. Later on Margaret married Will, and joined him on the horse and cart round, carrying an enormous basket, for environs were growing all the time.

The bakehouse at the back was very large and had two ovens, one above the other, the fire at the side to heat the water (a steam bakery) fed by coke which Mr Hicks fetched from St Austell Gas works in his cart. The steel floor of the oven was cleaned every day with a malkin, a hessian bag wrapped round the end of a very long pole.

'Looking like a malkeen' was not a complimentary simile; Mother used it often.

Mr Hicks and Charlie baked a large part of what the population ate. 'Twas ½d for a tart, 1d for a big loaf, 1d for a dinner, (2d on Sundays) and 6d for a turkey on Christmas Day. A wealthy glutton complained once about that modest figure. Mr Hicks stood wielding the great shovel. Riding on it, out came a dinner from the cave, the name of its owner shouted aloud as it appeared. Johnny and Charlie knew the shape of everybody's dish, and if dishes were alike recognised the way potatoes and pastry were cut and arranged.

'Charlie, is this mine?'

'No, here's yours.'

Mr Meek, the plumber made little steel markers for some people, but in their usual haphazard fashion, not many bothered; we never did. There would sometimes be mistakes, and then nobody would ever take a substitute. If it was too late to recover their own, a rejected dinner was left to get cold.

In the afternoon Charlie had a rest, and tins of pasties and tarts were left out for late comers to collect. There were never as many pennies left as items collected, but cynicism didn't bite very deep into Charlie. He knew perfectly well who it was hadn't paid.

When the baking was finished, people came and drew off

hot water for scrubbing their boats or front steps and brought clothes to dry in the great room above the bakehouse. Yes, the Hickses tolerated all this.

There was a time when Marj was put on to a course of Virol to try and get some flesh on her bones, and Charlie used to weigh her every week on the great scale. 'Come on, Marj, my handsome we'll see how you're doing, not fat enough yet.'

There remains to be told what services, all unpaid, Tom, Sam and Will performed for the country folk on whom they called.

First medicines. Dr Ross (Dr Grier's successor) visited outlying farms, prescribed, and then dispensed from the crenellated house at the top of Tregoney Hill. Will would walk up there to collect various bottles for delivery. On one occasion a visitor accosted him. 'Do you know this is a private drive, my man?' I'm sorry I wasn't there to rap out the retort Will was too mild to offer.

Then you'd see Sam struggling through the town with an accumulator which had been charged at Deeley Mann's, and parcels of fresh fish from Pawlyn's under his other arm. They even shopped for wool at John Farran's with requests to match up for colours! Methylated spirit was carried in large bottles from Mr Way's and cotton wool borne in bulk from the chemists. Margaret was given letters to post by a resident at Portmellon and asked to go to the post office, stamp them, and have the cost appended to the bill. 'I don't need any bread today thank you.' Lastly the footgear of the countryside was brought home in Tom's van for repair at Alfie Whatty's. On Monday mornings bearing mended shoes and account Alfie would appear in the shop and meet Tom at the desk. Tom actually paid the account there and then, but alas, like Charlie with his pennies he was often let down, not recovering his debts.

Carrie and Gladys are alive at the time of my writing. Gladys is the mother of Jonathan Barron, World Amateur Snooker Champion for 1970. In the thirties she lost her oldest child Billie aged eight. They laid straw the whole length of Church Street to prevent any noise disturbing the little boy. Gladys, without recovering, for there are those with hearts too

Long lining on the *Ibis,* Percy Hunkin, Dick Lakeman and
Eddie Lakeman pulling the line.

Launching the Lifeboat

St Austell County School

The Street, Mevagissey.
Three outside the Ship Inn.

tender to heal, has survived, still to be supporting whoever of her friends and relatives is in trouble. Like a certain great lady of whom I have read she is 'defective in egotism'.

Opposite Hicks' shop is the long side wall of Ship Inn against the middle of which stood the town pump. The Ship is a very old inn, and by virtue of size and central position the most important in Mevagissey. In our time it was run by Lil Barron, her mother, and brother George.

Lil, very large and light, carried herself like a queen, with an unconscious grace, a calm confidence, justified by her figure, her wit, her looks, and splendid capabilities. She took size 3 only in shoes, and on those little feet danced with joyful elegance, captivating the crowd at the Town Hall.

She and her mother worked like slaves keeping that rambling old Inn in perfect order. Gladys tells me that the curtains began to come down in January when they entered upon the ritual of spring-cleaning and a thorough spring-cleaning it was too, every floor-board scrubbed, all the corners scoured, no cover but what was washed, no single surface left unwhitened. Visitors to the Ship stepped into a shining domain. Carrie and Gladys saw it all going on from their front bedroom window.

In our early days St George's Square had no need of a War Memorial and the oldest of the village architecture filled the space the memorial now occupies. It was so old, it fairly crumbled under your gaze but oh! so interesting and for those of us with a sense of history very precious. Tommy Thomas had his old shop there, and Mrs Rowe's bakehouse gave off a warm comforting smell at the side door where pottery without aroma has taken over.

What is now William Robins's butcher's shop was John Farran's high class grocer's and men's outfitters. The odd roll of lino and a few straw hats made a fringe for the groceries. John Farran was as wide as his great counter, and his dignified demeanour not often disturbed. He went for a walk, his constitutional on the quays every day, glad I imagine to get away from groceries and tailoring and to meet and talk with friends. He took short steps, crossing the square towards the harbour with eagerness. He had aspirations unrelated to his means of livelihood, being very interested in public life. John was definitely a subject for Dickens, enigmatic, dry, solidly ensconced in the nineteenth century. Conservative without arrogance, cautiously benevolent, very thoughtful.

The fruit in his shop resided in thick narrow but deep wooden drawers with gilt lettering on them, different drawers for different grades but they used to say there was precious little difference in any of it so you might as well buy the cheapest. You got middle class extras there, olives and pickled walnuts, things to which we didn't aspire! Then there was a huge basket of dried cod, large grey pieces which they called tow-rags. I suppose somebody ate it and found it good?

The class system for John was as unalterable as the weather, but I am sure he looked at society with an objective eye, and that all his judgements were well considered. Upper layers in Mevagissey were mercifully and innocuously thin, and certainly not reverenced.

Henry Varcoe's small grocery and greengrocery shop was what is now Clifton's his son's, much modernised. Clifton married Valerie Kendall, sister to Ena, Marjorie's childhood friend. We were often at the Kendalls' shining welcoming cottage in Church Street where there was a piano and a gramophone for Frank was very musical.

Valerie played 'Destiny' and 'Nights of Gladness' and Granny Matthews gave us nuts out of the patch pockets of her black apron. Frank and Mrs Kendall smiled on us all with benevolence, and our delight in the warm life of that cottage was not marred by any foreknowledge that dear Ena would die young.

What is now the Post Office was Mrs Barbary's great stone-floored shop which I always associate with chestnuts, since Eddie helped himself to one such tempting trifle from the top of a basket, and was sent to bed without his tea as a punishment for stealing, a crime less prevalent than now.

The life of Willie Cloke's shop, a general stores, was subordinated to charabancs and time-tables, which took Willie out and about. He had inherited movement from his father who owned the horse-buses, and he walked almost as fast as La Premiers and Endeavour ran, darting about the streets like a dragon-fly. At the wheel he was superbly capable and confident.

Up the street was Charlie Retallack's the butcher's. Charlie was tall, and cavalier, with a loud voice and not dedicated to cuts of meat any more than John Farran was to cuts of suits. Attentive to the children, he softened, bending down to ask 'What does your mother want, my handsome?' We started shopping when we were three.

Charlie was noted for excellent sausages available on certain days after 12 a.m. Hartley tells me he would be there at noon, but sometimes had to wait in a state of fatigued suspense until well after 1 p.m. before the sausages appeared. It was the price you had to pay for quality and Charlie adopted a take it or leave it attitude. People speculated about the recipe, one of those trade secrets never plumbed, but Mrs Dunn, Jack's mother, discovered a clue. She had a shop opposite and Charlie bought ground rice there on the mornings of those days when sausages were manufactured. Was this the Retallack unknown ingredient? If so in what proportions was it included?

Charlie's eldest son Cyrus, very handsome, was a great footballer. We remember seeing him carried shoulder-high through Victoria Square after some spectacular triumph, his imperial name justified. He had a commission in the army, and it was on his tall ample frame we first saw the uniform of an officer, top grade.

Opposite the Backlet Opening was Mr Way's (Jim's) Hardware Store which he combined with a bicycle agency and hiring service. The fee to hire a boneshaker was 6d a day which payment was often eaten up in unpaid repairs, for the unscrupulous left machines with punctured tyres in the passage at close of day. Down that long passage to the right of the shop, I often edged my way, past all the two-wheeled patients calling for Ruth at the side-door. She and I used to sing duets together in chapel, Ruth treble, and I alto.

Willie, the eldest son and an asthmatic, was always at home and on duty. I can hear his husky voice as I write. So patient he was and obliging, and Mrs Way who had such bright eyes and curly hair cared for him so. He died young.

The boys used to chant 'Where there's a Will, there's a Way, Where there's a Way there's a bike,' and then Myrtle married Mr Ryder, so another line was added.

When Fernley succeeded to his father's business, he carried on the family tradition of patching up everything for everybody without complaint. 'Ask Fernley, he'll do that for you.' There never was a nail whatever the length he couldn't find, an electrical repair he couldn't tackle, a piece of wire he was unable to supply, the small payment being quite disproportionate to the service.

Martin, his brother, has only recently died, and he baked good wholesome bread for the community in a little Cliff Street bakery, exchanging drolleries over the counter as extras.

Another bakery up Church Street was Joey Over's. Joey, Ernie, Mabel and Lily worked together in that miniature building, four busy floury figures. We bought sweets at Joey's on the way to school, a ha'path or penneth of snowballs, toffee globes covered in sherbet, served by Mabel in a cone-shaped packet. You licked off the sherbet first, and then sucked the globe making it last up the hill. I associate snowballs with the ringing of the school-bell.

Marj used to collect coins from the Coronation mugs on the boys' bedroom mantelpiece. They fell out of their trouser pockets and were deposited in the mugs behind the faces of George V and Mary. We were allowed these pickings for services rendered. The mugs, the coloured faces, crowns and contents added up to a monarchy romantic, pictorial, and profitable.

Alfie and Willie Whatty had a shoemaker's shop at the bottom of Cliff Street, a small shack still there, with a large window. Little men they sat facing it, side by side, each over an iron foot, and surrounded by bits of leather and tacks, firmly fastened to the bench by a self-imposed discipline also of iron. An occasional lightning movement took one of them to the side where a machine buzzed to make edges smooth.

Your shoes were always well repaired and ready on time for the Whatties had method. There was no wasting of words, and they didn't even stop work while you described what you wanted done. I'm sure they made and repaired footgear for two lifetimes each, for they both lived to be very old, Willie only recently having died.

Alfie used his short legs to achieve a resolute stride much longer than many a tall man would ever dream of attempting. He had a beautiful purple clematis over the archway that led to his front door up Polkirt, probably the only one in old Mevagissey, and its prestige rubbed off on to its owner. Alfie also followed up his purposeful walk with the purchase of a car quite early on, and reached London in it getting inextricably bound up in Piccadilly Circus. Willie did a part time job as postman so that he had a second channel of insight into personality. I wonder whether he found any correspondence between frequency and character of mail, and shape and tread of feet?

Many of the women suffered in their feet, like old Mrs Prynn whose every utterance had for a coda 'Oh! my poor feet.' Passing over the Town Bridge with a small piece of steak on the palm of her outstretched hand she cried 'Sixpenneth o'meat for my great family. Oh! my poor feet.'

And there was he who complained so much, that his confidant, running short of cures for bad feet said, 'Have ee tried washing 'em?'

John Beer and his single son John also made and repaired boots and shoes, their workshop being the front room of a terrace-house in Church Street, first door on the left as you went in. John was tall and big, his large face and black apron shining in the same way, the hair on his head falling straggly round his ears. Very gentlemanly were John and his family, sensitive folk and sad. Florrie, the single housekeeper daughter, would sometimes appear out through the long passage.

Temperamentally unsuited to the circumstances from which they hadn't the power to escape, they put a brave smiling face on a life that must have been dull and hard, and did good honest work.

I seem to remember that the Beers were musical, that there was a capacity for culture there. I only know for certain that as I stepped out of the front door, shoes under my arm, and

saying, 'Goodbye, Mr Beer. Thank you very much. Goodbye.'
I was aware of a great sadness. It would take a Turgenev to do
justice to that household, to capture the particular pathos
which prevailed.

The last little shop up Church Street was Mrs Beswarick's
which had a domestic window only, and high steps to reach
the door. It was very dark inside and full of everything, but
chiefly vegetables.

Claudie used to deliver vegetables from a cart, and Joe ran
round, a small schoolboy, in his dinner-hour carrying a big
basket. How the children did work to be sure, and especially
those of long families.

Claudie is alive and keen still. The Beswaricks were richer
in wit and philosophic calm than in worldly goods, and
Claudie, a staunch member of the Congregational Church,
has always been an observant assessor of character and
situation. She loves words and writes verses about the life of
the church to which she has contributed so much.

VII

St Austell County School

Many of us followed Ann Treneer (author of *School House in the Wind*) and A.L. Rowse (famous historian) to St Austell County, grafting a little grammar school culture on to our Cornish temperaments, and taking home its outward signs in second-hand text-books.

The two storeyed granite building, small, square and solid looking, was then complete in itself and had a friendly domestic appearance. A door was a door in those days, and not an ill-defined part of the general facade. Bushes shielded us from the road, and natural hedges surrounded the playing field on the Tregonissey side. Down the hill towards the town and very near, stood the Brewery.

From the front at the top we looked out through trees and across fields bespattered with houses of every variety to St Austell Bay and Fowey Stack. At the start I secured a seat in a corner of the back row, and felt safe as long as the sea was visible. It seemed so very far away, two whole miles as the crow flies, maybe. That is what comes of being born with the waters on your doorstep, and the roar of an ocean in your ears.

The brewery emitted a powerful stench at regular intervals, and the density of the air increased so as to make of physics and chemistry comprehensible sciences; beer became the very element in which we lived and learned. It got mixed up with feudalism, Gladstone, isosceles triangles, Latin verbs, Palgrave's *Golden Treasury* and all the zones.

My cousin Hartley Pollard, preceding me by three years, remembers on his first day at St Austell seeing Rowse, then in the VIth form making entries on the notice board. The intriguing thing was that the writing stood out, not by reason of size or style, but the fact that it moved between, rather than on the lines, which unusual position gave it an arresting quality. When the tall fellow strode down the corridor, ignoring the motley crowd, Hartley knew that there was someone storing future notoriety for himself in the recesses of his proud head, and the small awe-stricken boy was reminded of those 'lexicon-minded' clerics outside Truro Cathedral, a picture of whom he had seen in his Great Uncle Harris's book.

Soon after I came to the County School there was a stir in the air, and an important announcement from the platform concerning an old boy who had become a 'Fellow of All Souls'. What that meant was a mystery to me. It had an ecclesiastical sound, and there was obviously honour in it. I made no display of my ignorance, deciding that this was one of many matters I could safely leave to time to unravel. We were given a day off, and the flag flew with a Tregonissey flutter on the school flagstaff, so that my introduction to the name of Rowse had associations of gratitude, a holiday enjoyed at his expense, and a boost for the humble establishment into which I had involuntarily drifted. The Education Act bore one of its early fruits when an academic gene in Rowse's inheritance surfaced and blossomed in the fastnesses of the Clay District.

County School for us was an outpost of Mevagissey, and how fortunate that it should be a co-educational Establishment with a headmaster and mistress, Mr Barritt and Miss Bond, who approved of the set-up. In the cosmopolitan society of the St Austell area, which included the whole of the Clay District, we remained a separate group with a distinct identity which no amount of mixing could modify. We associated freely during dinner hours, not with the town children, who went home at mid-day, and many of whom were much grander than we, but with boys and girls from outlying parts, the children of the 'Higher Quarters'. They had a different accent from ours which I secretly thought very quaint. A friend tells me that the Mevagissey accent was the most marked of any! We were united in a lack of polish, an innocence, a wildness tempered by gentleness, a naïveté streaked with shrewdness.

At their best the Cornish are very courteous, obliging and considerate; at their worst impetuous, undisciplined, stubborn, and unco-operative. Well we were all these things by turn I dare say, and the staff must surely have been baffled dealing with a species so strange. Maybe it was sometimes more than we deserved to have such a democratic liberal headmaster who treated us with affectionate tolerant understanding. Mr Barritt (W.V.B.) loved Mevagissey for itself, and still more for providing him with Howard Dunn, who as a powerful Governor supported him in whatever liberal policies he instituted and pursued. Howard's motives could not have been entirely unmixed. I suspect that he enjoyed upsetting business magnates and clerics, and that the wildness in him was often uppermost. He was full of daring, but genuine and a visionary, which was exactly what Mr Barritt needed. Partly because of Howard, we were all expected to be bright, and perhaps sometimes we were. At least we were 'different'.

Ten years ago W.V.B. then over eighty, told me of the Mevagissey boy, who one night arrived at the door of his house in Poltair Road with an offering of fresh fish. He had come after dark so as not to be seen, and refused to reveal his identity lest he be suspected of currying favour. It was enough that the headmaster should know that Mevagissey thought well of him, and was showing it with an offering of their peculiar asset – FISH.

I remained at St Austell for six years, and throughout that time had not one unhappy moment occasioned by school. Ours was a good class made up of St Dennis, Foxhole, Trethorgey, Roche, Bugle and Tregonissey boys and girls, and a few of the St Austell bourgeoisie.

The chief difficulty for us in those days was travel, and when I started in the early twenties, in the absence of a convenient bus, we all rode bicycles. Peggy Maher, Dinny's daughter, had a Raleigh, and I had a Swift. Mine was the taller with black handlebars, a Utility article designed like clothes, for growing.

Arch, my second brother, a great one for assuming responsibility, taught me to ride at the top of Tregoney Hill,

Lane End, where stinging nettles flourish, and into a small forest of which I overturned. 'Come on,' he cried, 'git up, thass nutheen, keep gaween.' And I did. 'Now then. Right. Good.'

Arch had very deep grey eyes which spoke. Always susceptible to the cold I used to sit with my feet on the fender of the Cornish range to do my homework for the most part unnoticed by everyone except Arch. He did so approve of sticking at it, and entering the glass door of the kitchen would give me a quick loving glance and commendatory nod.

Our bicycles became part of us. They had personalities of their own, akin to their owners, and the wheels turned in a kind of companionship on a twin journey. Once up the hill, and out of Mevagissey, the road was easy, and we sped down to Pentewan without fear of traffic, blessed by the sun, battered by the wind and drenched by the rain. Then there was the dawdling for others to catch up, and along the Moors we travelled often five and six abreast, sometimes gazing quietly ahead or aloft, at other times laughing and arguing. We became careless, too slow, too talkative, abstracted, inattentive. One or two lost their balance and we all toppled and fell in a tangle of machines. The clock wasn't waiting for us, but we weren't chastised if late. The regimen was flexible, allowing a margin for human fallibility which never seemed to undermine our essential trustworthiness.

Hartley was the only one of us to speak quite correctly and musically. He says it was deliberate, because he felt it necessary in order to earn a living in the only sphere accessible to him, but I believe it was something deeper, an aesthetic sensibility which affected his ear and voice-box.

Jack Dunn (Cap'n Eckey's grandson) and Peter Hunkin, two years older than me, could have been our grandfathers. Jovial, relaxed, and smilingly tolerant of our extreme youth they were never afflicted by learning but none the less able for that. Homework was an incidental in those days, not the crippling tyranny it has become for so many adolescents now. It grieves me to see their personalities warped by such a compelling competitive convention.

So our bicycles allowed us freedom, fresh air, conversation, good company, or a solitary ride if we wanted it. I have memories of many a journey made quite alone in the magic of early morning, and the hush of evening, with time and space and peace in plenty, and nature in all her moods for company. Events of the day fell into perspective, and human affairs took their place as a small part only of a mysterious and wonderful creation. I always loved the promise of 'In my house are many mansions' and the colloquial assurance of 'If it were not so I would have told you.' I wouldn't want a mansion bigger nor smaller than the heart of Mevagissey sixty years ago, nor a drive longer, shorter nor different in any particular from the road that led from St Austell home. Listen to the names, Moorland Road, Iron Bridge, London Apprentice, Tallack's Corner, Nansladron, Pentewan, Tregiskey, Trewinney. Mornings and evenings the year through that road wound itself into the convolutions of our brains, so that every tree, every bush, the tall hedges, the little fields, the ferns and all the flowers the indentations of the coast, and the gushing white river became so familiar as to be an extension of ourselves. It was a close ecological partnership in which we merged with nature wild and tender, bleak and burgeoning, angry and smiling, a parent whose innocent children we were, without consciousness then of large-scale cruelty, or painful private doubts.

In the distance stood the sandheaps etched against the sky on the edge of the world. They represented everything romantic and exotic, exhilarating and unexplored. The meadowsweet sprang luxuriant on the banks of the clay-river, and willow-herb ran riot in the marshy fields. Never did foxglove rise more majestically than in those crowded hedges, nor honeysuckle smell sweeter than on Pentewan Old Hill. I took bunches of it to Edith when she was near her end, and she held the smooth pink stems in her thin hands, and gazed into infinity.

There was the omnipresent gorse too which could well be the Cornish emblem, brilliant, prickly, and prolific, penetrating the senses with its coconutty scent. It took over hedge and bank flourishing with a vitality careless of space or competition, and opening with a golden glory that defies both change and death.

During my first year at school Mavis Dunn, Jack's sister, then in the fifth form was my guardian. I called for her at her house in the front street, went up the stairs into the room over the shop, and sat by the fire. Mrs Dunn would be bathing the youngest of her six boys, Stephen. She was calm and unhurried, and in a sense detached from the multitudinous tasks she had to perform. Never crippled by the trivial, she provided a comment on affairs of the day, and had a personal word of encouragement for us all, while the boys one by one went off to school. Mavis has remained a friend to this day: Unassuming and shy, she has an independent spirit splashed with wide streaks of humour. Re-reading Jane Austen regularly she chuckles in such a way as would make the heart of that dear lady glad.

One or two incidents on the road come back to me. We had been having examinations and a history paper had provided me with opportunity to express some thoughts of a political nature, inspired by my father's talk. Mr Martin, our history master, who loved his subject, bent over my shoulder as I was doing arithmetic, to tell me how pleased he was with what I had written. All day I waited to go home to tell my father how right he was, and that evening, tired, happy and quite alone I was free-wheeling along Moorland Road after a 'swift' descent of the hill when I lost consciousness and fell from my bicycle. Some kind gentleman, (a visitor), in a large open car, picked up me and my bicycle and took us both home. I 'came to' outside Hicks's shop on the Town Bridge to hear Uncle Ambrose who happened to be passing, asking the driver what he thought he was up to, knocking me down. The gentleman was later found and with generous and amused understanding accepted apologies and heartfelt thanks.

From about 1925 onwards Mr Willie Cloke's bus took children to school. Numbers were increasing, and several parents began paying the fee that allowed entrance to the grammar school. I think it was £3 a term. On very wet windy days, we sometimes left our bicycles at home and boarded the charabanc (ch as in chat). It was a shaky affair of it, a piece of canvas stretched over a few seats on four wheels. You raised the flaps which were windows if the weather was fine, and huddled in the centre when it was raining. The driving was good, and we were relatively safe. Later on when the Western National took over, Ernie Behennah was the conductor. His was the thankless task of keeping order when spirits ran excessively high, and annoyed the few adults who were passengers along with us. Once on the way home as we were nearing Pentewan, Ernie became so exasperated he turned every one of us, innocent and guilty alike out of the bus, and we had to walk the last two miles in the wet and windy twilight.

Ernie had a healthy scorn for blazers, badges, ties and school caps, and told us as much in no uncertain terms. Manners he shouted were more important than book learning. We were very fond of Ernie but the boys and one or two of the girls set out to provoke him, because his fiery temper was so entertaining, and his epithets so pertinent. He was a master of histrionics.

Ernie later married and his daughters have grown up to distinguish themselves, one to become a doctor who is now practising in Mevagissey, and another who has taken a degree course at London University. Unhappily Ernie didn't live to see them through their careers, but they were doing well at school before he died. The Behennahs all had something extra.

Then there was the time when the charabanc rounding the bend at the bottom of Poltair Road emptied Marj flat on her back out of the very high door. She was leaning against it there being no room further in. Through the window I saw her land in the road, her limbs seeming to have parted company with her trunk. She was unconscious for about twenty-four hours, but is still here, and as sound in mind as anyone else.

Another day Peggy Maher and I sat together in the bus going home waiting for the rumbling start of the engine. There was a pleasant hum of voices. We were engaged in earnest subdued conversation without any hint of disputation, concerning the different methods we had used in the solving of a knotty arithmetical problem. The question paper lay on our knees. It amounted almost to an exchange of temperaments while each deferred to the other with due respect. Then one gentle hand fell on Peggy's right and another on my left shoulder and a voice which I recognised as Mrs Picken's said, 'Don't stop. I want to go on listening to you.' Her face was all alight. Mrs Picken was the gracious beautiful ex-teacher whom I have described in another place as the minister's wife. Do adults always realise I wonder what a powerful influence they exercise when they have mastered the art of supporting the young without intrusion?

We had several young teachers at the St Austell County School, most of them pleasant and capable. Mr Barritt himself was the original one; he regarded us thoughtfully and as individuals wondering always how we should be taught and seeking the right approach. Never did he shut himself off as headmasters of large establishments have a way of doing now in these 'enlightened' days. He moved among us continually, and appeared in all classrooms to take lessons and sometimes to sit down and talk to us.

By training he was I think a mathematician and in everyday life a philosopher. I remember his giving us a lesson on the infinitesimal which held me spellbound. I thought of it when later I came to read some of Einstein's prose. If only we could have approached physics and other branches of science in this way, how much better educated most of us would be.

Mr Saunders was from Bude and a Methodist, as was Mr Parsons, and they used to preach sometimes in our Mevagissey chapel and give papers at the Guild. I could never quite reconcile their secular aspect with the solemn bearing they wore in the pulpit. Dual personalities such as this bothered me, and sermonising teachers invalidated education and Christianity alike. Besides it didn't do mixing up teachers with parents: they were races apart.

Mr Saunders was better on the Sports Field where his athletic figure showed up well in cream flannels and smart pullover, and his curly head looked so handsome. The modernity and the elegance were quite stunning; it was our little bit of Eton. It wasn't Eton though nor Harrow neither, when Mr Saunders played the piano with such Non-Comformist fervour, weightiness only possible in a Wesleyan.

Mr Richardson had a fund of tolerance which qualified him

to deal with the young, even though they were Cornish. When in middle age I met him again, I remembered how kindly and intelligent he always had been. As for Mr Martin it was he who inspired me to read history. Quite formidable, he never failed to give praise when it was due, and he cared about history even in the classroom! We didn't fare badly. A lot of it was dull, but what school was ever equipped with an entirely good staff?

Hermia Lillicrap remembers Mr Martin giving them an English lesson on the Verb To Be. She was ten and had come to St Austell with an early scholarship. It was fascinating she tells me, but unfortunately she had no idea what this particular grammatical structure was. Strange: The Verb To Be (and all its parts) – something mysterious in the arcana of higher education. We would sometimes have science teachers take odd lessons outside their province. Hermia remembers one young lady reading with them from Scott's *Marmion*. While not approving of the choice, she says she quickly became aware that she understood Sir Walter's lines far better than did her teacher.

As for mathematics Mr Lodge told us how simple it all was, and I did admire the beautiful unintelligible hieroglyphics on the blackboard, but alas the comprehension thereof had to be left chiefly to the boys, and a very few girls who were fortunate enough to have mathematics in their bloodstream. I arranged my desk in the corner so that I was able to pass long periods of algebraical and geometrical time reading novels or history. I somehow knew that equations and theorems had a beauty akin to poetry, but decided that my inner eye was in this splendid direction quite blind, and made no attempt to find any spectacles.

We hadn't a library at our grammar school, but were allowed to wander into the town in the dinner hour, and there was a musty room in South Street where I gathered up George Eliot and Thomas Hardy. *Adam Bede* I found as near as anything that ever was to the *News of the World*, and Maggie Tulliver had already become a close friend.

As for Tess, poor dear Tess, I had to repair to Tregoney Hill attic to weep over her fate.

At the end of our assembly hall was a bookcase with glass doors which were rarely opened, the shelves full of Everyman copies of the classics. Howard Hooper my contemporary, explored this treasure-house, and pointed out to me Dostoievsky on the top shelf. 'You should be reading *Crime and Punishment*, Mary,' he said, 'and not delaying.' I saw Hooper many years later, by which time I had made almost complete acquaintance with the Russians. It wasn't of them that we talked however, but of ourselves. He told me how he had passed much of his time at Oxford adapting to a foreign culture, learning all the tricks as he put it. I confessed that at Bristol I had failed almost before I began, to accommodate to the bourgeoisie. Here I was, still in firm possession of accent, prejudices, shyness and aggression, an incurable obdurate Celt.

There is a sort of working class cult at the moment which I don't altogether trust. Experience has taught me that it fails to function when it should best operate. However things are certainly much easier than they were half a century ago, unless perhaps age irons out social difficulties, and a lot of other nonsense as well.

Our text books were heavy, well worn, and almost entirely without illustrations. The type was small and black, and the end of every volume looked a million light years away from the take-off. There was no pandering to entertainment I fear; we had to entertain each other. Mr Barritt did his best for us, and I remember there was some system instituted by him for the inexpensive hiring of books.

You lifted the lid of your desk and removed a dingy tome for 'silent reading', or a book of exercises to find the page where you had left off. The action was automatic when certain teachers entered the room, and an important part of our conditioning.

We studied one Shakespeare play a year, and ended up with *King Lear* and *The Tempest* in the VIth form. I once turned on the Radio at home to revise *Twelfth Night* while doing homework. When Andrew Aguecheek and Toby Belch came on the air, Mother, immediately on the alert said, 'Whatever is all that?'

'Shakespeare,' I replied, 'for an exam.'

'What a lot of trash,' she cried, with an authority equal to Tolstoy's. 'Turn it off for goodness sake. If that's Shakespeare, I don't think much of it.'

We took such a long time to get through books in class. It was very tedious. *The Wind in the Willows* blew for a whole year, and I have wished many times that Longfellow had kept Hiawatha, along with Minnehaha, Nokomis and the rest to himself.

It was a diet that modern children would reject outright. We were thankful for 'Sohrab and Rustum', *The Splendid Spur*, *Silas Marner* and *Barchester Towers*, but not so for *Wild Wales* and *Rob Roy*. Reading for enjoyment was largely extraneous to the syllabus. How we'd have loved paper-backs!

In the sixth form we had precious little tuition, about four lessons a week at most, and there was only one other girl besides myself. We used a small room at the back of the new School-hall.

The *Letters of Erasmus* was a Latin set-book, unfortunately without a key. Eastertime had arrived, and we hadn't even started it. I spent the whole holiday, morning, noon and night working out what Erasmus had said in those letters, and writing up a translation. That the good man had done so much translation himself made of it a fitting exercise, and he would I am sure have looked kindly on my efforts. It was perhaps because I had been living in the light of his largeness during those weeks that I passed on my version of those letters complete to the other girl. She got a State Scholarship. I didn't. She didn't need it. I did. But at least Erasmus was now part of my mental furniture, and I know he had had a hard time of it himself.

We had a choir in which I sang alto, and Miss Parry and Miss Lewis took us away to competitions which we never won. I was once reproved by Miss Lewis for pulling up my socks on the platform, but didn't know, so couldn't tell her then, that it was misplaced activity. Miss Lewis spent most of her French lessons hammering in English Grammar and chalking up neat compartments on the board for adverbical and adjectival extensions of predicates. The only thing to do was to study

ET-J

profiles and the sky, a waste of good French time but rewarding all the same. Until Charles de Gaulle died, I was able to follow simple sentences in French as he delivered them. Once we had a slender bright auburn-haired young lady with a degree in French who came for a while on supply. Her accent was startling, her features fascinating, her clothes very fashionable and it was all so exciting you felt like bursting out into the Marseillaise. As it was, we fairly raced through *Lettres de mon Moulin*. Had there been talk then of a Common Market I might have been converted to it.

On Sports Day she arrived on the field in an emerald green silk dress, and all the men of the staff, old and young, attached and unattached alike, crowded round her. They were transmogrified, and I swear they quite forgot their rôles as housemasters.

On Friday afternoon during the choir period Mr Barritt took the whole school for community singing in the hall. His enthusiasm knew no bounds, and he played the piano with gusto, but correctly and with fine feeling. His favourite song was 'Pretty Polly Oliver lay musing in bed'. I was always pleased if choir had to be cancelled so as to sing with the crowd. Even the boys gave vent, and lost their inhibitions.

W.V.B. also loved 'Snowy Breasted Pearl' but to his chagrin it evoked no response in us, and the singing was thin and half-hearted. 'Hands up those who don't like this song.'

All hands half up. 'But why oh why?'

The truth was we were embarrassed by the snowy breast. W.V.B. didn't realise that we used the word breast only in connection with 'breast of lamb' or 'breast of Lang' as one very genteel Mevagissey woman used to call it.

There were Speech and Prize Days too and I seem to remember Mr Barritt looking a bit glum on these occasions. Hermia reminds me that in the early days they were held at the Public Rooms in Truro Road, and that once Rowse came to present prizes. It was from him that she first heard the phrase 'havering and hovering' and he spoke on the same occasion about the brilliance of the British at improvisation. Perhaps it would have been better if we had known how to plan ahead?

Mr Barritt sent for me once and said, 'Look here, Mary, I've a few books left over. What about giving one of them to Marjorie?'

'But sir,' I said, 'she hasn't earned any prize.'

'What does that matter?' he retorted. 'I'm sure she'd like a book. We'll write in something; needlework will do.'

He didn't hear our Marj laugh, but oh how I wish he had. He and I must have felt the same about prizes even then. When during World War II a bomb fell on me and my few possessions, destroying the books I had won as prizes in school, (including a complete Shakespeare bound in black leather) I ruefully admitted to myself that here was the poetic justice after which I had always yearned. Why should I shed a single tear? But who will not forgive me remembering the feel of that beautiful leather binding, and treasuring the memory with all its associations?

Once the great Quiller Couch came to present our books to us. He delivered a fine speech, the content of which I cannot remember. What a splendid figure he made on the platform, handsome, ugly, and such a grand spotted bow as he wore. Robin Day could never achieve anything like it, for it needed Q's gnarled face and great head to set it off. Those blue eyes sparkled down on us, and never before nor since have I felt so proud of being Cornish.

There is no better book still for young readers than *The Splendid Spur*, captivating enthralling from beginning to end. Is there any other woman in literature to surpass Joan o' the Tor for common sense, wit, devotion and courage all combined in one splendid creature? We certainly have reason to be proud of Q, and when on a sparkling June day recently, in Hartley's boat, we passed up Fowey river by Q's house and on out to sea, I did so wish I could tell the good man how he had inspired us all those years ago. What I wonder did he make of our solemn faces?

I don't remember ever seeing a Mevagissey parent at a Speech Day or even a school play, and the Higher Quarters' parents didn't come either. There was no tradition in our village of parents visiting school, except sometimes in Mevagissey to complain about some undeserved punishment.

As for St Austell, they were too busy, too tired, disinclined to dress up and get the bus, and too shy also I suspect to enter that hall amongst their middle-class contemporaries who were so much more watchful of their children's academic progress. I am sorry they were never there, and that I didn't hear the remarks they would have made. I see in a possible row, the enigmatic faces of Jabie and Mrs Edwards, Walter and Mrs Dunn, Arthur and Mrs Pollard, Jimmy and Mrs Elvins, Joe and Mrs Lobb, Jim and Mrs Hunkin, Dinny and Mrs Maher, and my own father and mother older than the others, parents of children born 'at risk'.

When I consider it they were extraordinarily trusting and benevolent, and as long as we were happy asked few questions and made fewer demands. Reports hadn't become the ghastly obsession they amount to in these times. Ours were scanned and signed on the morning of the first day of term unearthed from the sideboard drawer, where they resided with the Methodist Plan and a few toffees.

Just before I left school W.V.B. said to me, 'Mary, why have I never seen your parents?' There was no simple answer: a whole culture would have had to be incorporated in a satisfactory reply.

No one knows much about the community life of a school unless he stays to dinner. I think I should make it compulsory for every Minister of Education to have a meal with the crowd at least once a month. (Mrs Thatcher, former Conservative Minister of Education, would certainly have had to remove whichever of her hats she was wearing.)

At St Austell Grammar there were two sittings, the first at 2/6d a week for a meal cooked on the premises, in a small building which looked like an outpost of the Brewery. The second was for those penurious or particular, who brought their own food and paid 6d a week for tea. I used to keep the books and collect all moneys on Monday mornings, my only incursion into accountancy, and I hope the Lord will excuse me such employment when tasks are allocated in heaven.

We had trestle tables covered with orange cloths which were dirty by Tuesday, and the hubbub was something awful. Food came from above in a lift worked by hand. Dear Alice

Bond, the headmistress, tried hard to civilise the proceedings, but achieved little. The boys used to put spares down on the seat beside them. Perhaps it was as well that Ernie Behennah didn't act as conductor here, or his scorn would have put an end to higher education. Eating over, relaxation followed. We had a grass tennis court in the front which was our Wimbledon, and a few old rackets were available. There we played a highly frivolous version of the game bringing us as much joy as any professional performances have ever given to stars or their admirers. Rackets followed balls over the net, and hangers-on searched for lost balls in the hedge. Jeanne Edwards, Lena Lobb, Verona Hunkin and Mabel Elvins will remember it all, and our Higher Quarters' friends cannot have forgotten the cry of 'Look out, Suzanne Lenglen now serving.' The mirth was so infectious it must have travelled far down the Tregonissey Road in the summer breeze.

Marjorie quite recovered from her dread of school, and put on flesh. Mother used to say that money was never better spent than on sending her to St Austell. When the dinner hour was wet, we gathered upstairs in one of the rooms, all of which were left open, and did impersonations. Members of staff might put a head round the door sometimes, the menfolk wearing quizzical expressions, hungry to know what was going on, and half afraid lest they find out.

It was there, when, already a prefect I drifted in to find Hermia Lillicrap, sitting with Jeanne and company among the audience, listening to Marj doing Miss Carrie Roberts conducting a round. Hermia came from Carpalla, Foxhole, and this was her introduction to life in that renowned place down by the sea, beyond Pentewan. She was small with large dark eyes, and big teeth in a round face framed with black shining hair. Her body was round too, and full of spring like her wits. The very epitome of youth, of joy in life and learning, her chuckle compassed every situation, while an extensive vocabulary resided behind her radiant countenance. 'Too poor you know, Mary, we were,' she has recently said to me, 'to know that we were poor.' What after all, did it matter that our gym slips hung down at the back and the pleats fell out because of the scantiness of the material? We were too happy, too companionable to be competitive, cushioned by the sublime confidence of innocence.

Hermia came to Mevagissey to see for herself what it was like and wasn't disappointed. I went to Carpalla and remember her mother's teas in that room looking out on to the sandheaps and Long Lane leading down to St Stephen-in-Brannel in the wooded valley below. There'd be cold pasty, splits and cream, and saffron cake. 'Eat up, Mary. Come on now, another split. It isn't self denial week.'

One Friday afternoon we were all summoned into the hall for such a lecture on behaviour as all schoolmasters feel bound to deliver now and then. Mr Barritt admonishing and pleading with restraint and reason had become oblivious of time, and the hands of the clock left 4 p.m. well behind. The Mevagissey crowd was at the very back near an easy exit. Marj became anxious, not only about the driver of our bus, but also to get home, and attacked by an end-of-week urgency, decided with a 'thass nuff o' that now' spirit to slip out. The rest of the Mevagissey contingent tiptoed after her. Then came a mighty voice: '*Stop: come back*, Marjorie Lakeman, walk up here please.'

With trembling lip and beating heart she passed down through the silent ranks, arrested now to a sharp and excited attention, Marj raised her head to the platform. 'Why were you leaving the hall before being dismissed?'

'Sir, the bus.'

'Ah the Mevagissey bus. Listen Marjorie, Never, never again must you dare to take the law into your own hands in such a fashion. Stop and consider what you are doing. And all you others, weakly following on. Remember my words. Foolish impetuous children. Go back now, Marjorie, and all of you stand still while I finish what I have to say.'

'Sir, I'm sorry, very sorry sir.'

Marj has wondered if her impulsive behaviour of so definite a subnormal nature had anything to do with being born in 1913 the year of the Mental Deficiency Act. She has a brisk reassuring manner with the many defaulters who have come her way over a lifetime of Welfare Work and like W.V.B. himself never fails to be aware of the 'innocence' of a large percentage of society's offenders.

Then too there was the occasion when 3Z had reached the dissecting stage in Biology and Marj brought a fish fresh from the salt sea for the purpose (volunteered I daresay). When the operation had been completed the teacher summoned her to the bench to decide whether the fish was still fit to be eaten. There was a roar of mirth at the lowering of the nose to the fish, and another at the slightly disdainful 'No certainly not' judgement of the connoisseur.

I imagine that the laughter had a note of derision for Mevagissey in it. The St Austellites would call our village Fishigissey with more than a hint of offensiveness, for they meant it to be pejorative. We retreated into haughtiness, but underneath were never all that sure of ourselves. Was there in fact something strange about us, some deficiency we were too stupid to recognise? Were we actually of different clay from the population of the Clay District?

By the time I had reached the Middle School, the building was sadly overcrowded. Chemistry and Physics Labs had to be used as form-rooms, and children traipsed about and sat on stools for lessons. Bunsen burners presided over the arts and sciences alike; at least there was no physical dichotomy in learning; Marj met the Bunsen Burner again when she trained as a nurse, and used it for testing of urine before the newer quicker method was adopted. It was like a face once ignored, and later become important, or meeting somebody with great joy in Australia one hadn't even noticed at home. Science did matter after all and education often has its beginnings in the slenderest of perceptions.

3Z got very restless sitting on stools, and when an ex-pupil came back on supply as a teacher, her high seriousness was too much for these spirited displaced adolescents. They were punished for their insubordination by having to come back on a Saturday morning for an academic session.

Marj went off swinging her worn hockey-stick as a foil, and when with forced gaiety, she tripped down the garden path, Mother, looking at me sharply said, 'Strange thing that! Hockey so early in the day. What's going on?' The careless shrugging of my shoulders, in an attempt to shield my young sister failed to put Mother off the scent. Sport didn't feature very largely for us in school-life, but we weren't thought the less of for that. Long journeys on bicycles in all weathers, and for me many duties at school, were very tiring. Besides which Mevagissey on a Saturday was a place you'd be foolish to leave if you could avoid it. I retreated from half-back to back, to goal in the hockey-team out of sheer exhaustion, and sacrificed prestige to comfort by secretly encouraging other aspiring contestants to take my place. Their gratitude quite bewildered me.

There were the enthusiasts of course, mostly St Austell girls from middle-class homes. They were beautiful creatures who sped across the field without sign of fatigue, and scored goals from the wings with a finesse that matched the cut of their clothes. I remember them so clearly, and the admiration I felt for skills outside my capacities.

The three Thomases, Eleanor, Millicent and Jennifer came from a big farm on the Truro Road, and the eldest, so Hermia tells me, once came to school in a shining pony-trap which she left in the yard of the White Hart.

Other beautiful girls, Mollie Stamp and Marjorie Piper starred in school plays, Quality Street and The Rivals. I once played in a humble one-act do as an Irish grandmother, and Mr Barritt coached me in the Irish accent which after all came out Cornish. I wore a black bonnet and cape and the scene came back to me when we were in Cork, and a student, having procured tickets walked with us to the theatre. The play was packed full of doubt which miraculously turned into faith at the end of the last scene.

We didn't go out of school very much on excursion or visits, except sometimes in the cause of botany. We trailed down town first and then up Mennycuddle Street, very steep, to a region overrun with old man's beard. It was a hoary spectacle indeed, and my whole being felt out-of-touch with nature in the straggling colourless guise it wore in that rough region. How much better to stay in school if only with Watts' School Flora for company. On those rough walks school-dinner resided in my weak stomach like a pile of pebbles.

Miss Rich, a very pretty amiable graduate, was our botany

mistress, and she married Mr Hill the English master, tall, handsome and flashingly dark. He once gave me full marks for an essay on *Silas Marner* wherein I remember ardently upholding Eppie's decision not to leave her dear father for a luxurious home.

I believe Miss Rich and Mr Hill were very happy, and I am very glad, though I didn't like the botany walks.

It was in the second half of the twenties that tragedy cast a deep shadow over us, and we suffered a shock that left us subdued and bewildered. Two of our number, a brother and sister called Jenkins, and the only children of a St Dennis schoolmaster were killed in a road accident, a rare occurrence in those days.

I went as one of a small band of seniors to the funeral. It was a grey day, and it seemed to me that the Clay District must be the saddest bleakest place in the whole world. This great sorrow was so crushing, and the sight of two coffins borne from the house, so excruciating, that the experience has remained with me ever since as a paradigm of insupportable pain. I learned on that dark day how fragile a thing is security, and how very much all our lives are at the mercy of chance. And still now that I am old, I am puzzled and distressed by the incongruity between dire undiscriminating circumstance, and the sensitivity of devoted discerning human beings.

All this was our school and how, when it was so fluid and flexible, so shapeless and imperfect, did it manage to leave such an indelible mark upon us? We developed willy nilly, not so much allowed to be independent as expected to be responsible for the self which no-one was silly enough to try and carry. It had a touch of A.S. Neill about it.

When the end came there was Mr Saunders with his Methodist zeal thundering away at the piano.

Forty years on when afar and asunder
Parted are those who are singing today.

And now more than forty years on I wonder what indeed we were really like in our work and our play?

I wept to leave my friends and most of the teachers, and to

see cut off that particular slice of time which terminated my childhood, a piece that had contained so much fun and hard work, and so little fear.

I feel sometimes I have forgotten everything I ever learned, but St Austell County made of me a student and by that I mean someone who must always be making an effort to understand what this life is all about.

I have a letter here from W.V.B. At ninety-one, he was remembering.

VIII

Food and Fashion

Women's magazines and a surfeit of cookery books have combined to harass most working women with aspirations they'd do better to drop. Preparation of food has become fussy and complicated, with the emphasis on refinements rather than on basics, the frantic search for variety resulting only in a standardisation which leaves no surprises in the regions. It is all part of the decadence of the Western world.

George Orwell, whose diaries have recently made of him an inmate of our house, and whom we lovingly call The Great Democrat, said way back in the forties that cottages produced better food than restaurants, and that people ought to be proud of their locality, and its cookery.

There was a time when we in Cornwall were reputed to live on pasties, which in a dietetic way explained our backwardness and insubordination. In the first place few English people know what constitutes a good pasty, and couldn't make one easily. Besides which we have only ever lived partially on pasties.

It was Dr Grier, that eminently sensible romantic, who, defending the pasty, set his seal upon it as a well-balanced, nourishing, appetising meal. The pastry must be thin and good, the meat tender and finely cut, (no mince thank-you), the potato, swede turnip and onion sliced small and paper thin, and the right proportion of butter, salt, flour, pepper and water wrapped up inside. Mother's were of the long slender variety with no lumps of pastry on the ends, and she curled them up in the same way as she ran downstairs, with a glide.

We ate fish two or three times a week. It might be fried ray curling at the edges, golden brown and succulent, or whiting boiled and served with butter and pepper, equally good of course, in its flaky delicacy, cooked in the frying pan. Pilchards were split and dried in the sun on a wooden board. Our cat never touched them; she'd already had a nice little gurnet, and serenely satiated, left our meal alone. The pilchards were 'roasted' on the gridiron over red-hot coals: you flicked them over by the tail and the fat was then in the fire. They put on a thin crust, and you ate them with your fingers. Mackerel had to be Joeys, a very small variety, and straight out of the sea. Their tender firm flesh, boiled for fifteen minutes or so, took well to vinegar and butter and pleased the discriminating stomach. Herrings yielded roes which were a meal in themselves, a dense mass of crumbling first-class protein.

Imagine the smell of roast pilchards on a fine winter afternoon when the fire glowed red in the Cornish range, and a red sun sank splendid in the sky. Roast pilchards, home-made bread, apple tart and cream, or perhaps date pasty, and plenty of hot tea from a brown shiny teapot with a fawn band around its middle; such was our fare.

On Saturday we always had boiled eggs and spice cake for tea. The spice cake was a mixture of apples, raisins, brown sugar, spice and breadcrumbs laid between the thinnest pastry and cut into squares. After which you found room for a saffron bun. Mother made bread twice a week, a large batch and we took it to the bakehouse, five cottage loaves. It was light, slightly salted, perfectly baked, and with just the right depth of crust.

And what of dinners? Small pieces of steak were curled in with a little fat and onion in the centre, floured, salted and peppered, placed in a shallow dish with some water, and potatoes, whole if small, or cut into chunks if large, placed on top a piece of fat laid over them. 'Scrowling up' in the beneficent heat of the oven the fat bathed the floury potatoes. A thick piece of pastry often resided at one end. The quality of the dish depended of course on the times. It wasn't the cook's fault if the potatoes had nothing but water for company.

Then there was turnip and potato pie, equivalent to a pasty for content, but with pastry on top of the dish only. We had broth with every sort of vegetable, and lentil soup made with marrow bones. Stew with lamb or beef and suet dumplings, the potatoes cooked separately appeared frequently. I still make the old brand of stew, and it is consumed with a sort of gusto and plates scraped perfectly clean. It's the consistency of stew that's so important, isn't it? We also had boiled brisket or shin with vegetables cooked whole and suet pudding as fortifier.

We particularly liked apple dumplings with cloves dropped in, and tapioca pudding wearing a nutmeg-flavoured buttery skin which slid down easily.

Mother bottled gooseberries and blackcurrants, and she lightly salted pounds of butter in large earthenware jars, and put eggs down in water-glass for times when they became scarce. We had blackcurrant tart for tea on Sundays, but it is a heavy fruit for delicate stomachs, and along with cream, made me feel very melancholy an hour or so later when we were singing 'The sands of time are sinking' in chapel. I'm afraid 'the dawn of heaven' was slow to break. A strict diet became necessary for me when the cares of working days accumulated. I live now vicariously on memories of more substantial days. (I remember walking slowly back from a funeral once with a male cousin of the same slight build as myself. We condoled with each other on the state of our digestions reduced to a ruinous condition by emotional disturbance, and were having recourse then to Slippery Elm Food.)

We ate yeast cake, and no sweet stuff, throughout the week, saffron and white, and were allowed a new bun off the wire tray. If there were any stale cake left when the new appeared, Father would cut it up and give everyone the same small amount, thereby avoiding waste and securing justice. Saffron cake usually had currants, and white, sultanas. Arch always used to turn his bun round and round scrutinising it before he took the first bite. Why we never discovered. There was sweet seed cake on Sundays.

Then at Easter-time a rice cake got beaten up, fatless and containing a large number of eggs. There emerged one of those flat-topped beautiful creations in a delicate yellow with a golden crust about ¼in. thick breaking towards the edges in pieces, which you surreptitiously removed if you dared. Black cakes heralded the approach of Christmas.

There was always a 2-lb. tin of Lyle's Golden Syrup on the table, in which we bathed our bread and butter. Eaten with cream it was called 'thunder and lightning'; we loved the green and yellow of that tin, and the splendid lion. Marj tells me she would repeat that line over to herself as she dipped in her spoon. 'Out of the strong came forth sweetness.' We loved all labels, and read them diligently. There was that nice turbanned Indian on the Camp Coffee bottle, the only coffee we ever saw, and which we rarely used. We drank Indian tea very hot, and strong enough to be stimulating. No sugar.

Then, of course, there was the 'lowance bag to be packed. Four men had to be provided with food for perhaps twenty-four hours. 'We'll have the 'lowance now then Mother. The wind has changed.' In would go loaves, butter, cheese, cold meat, yeast cake, apples and whatever else there was. Bad weather would often drive them in again with scarcely any of the food touched. I've seen my Mother patiently unpacking that bag four or five times in succession within a week.

We used to be sent to Mr Kemble's (Jimmy) the chemist's for hard liquorice. It came in round half-inch sticks, and we had it in the spring or whenever Mother considered it was good for our systems. She liked it herself. It made the teeth black.

Father's sister Henrietta went away as cook-housekeeper in a hostel for the assistants of Seccombe's stores in Cardiff. They greatly appreciated her food, but what astounded Mr Seccombe was that at the end of the quarter she always returned a substantial amount of the money she had been allowed. That economy could accompany quality and plenty was a phenomenon which baffled him. The truth is that our forebears were practised in the elimination of waste, and developed the sort of judgement that always made the best of what was available.

Fashion was an almost irrelevant factor during the bad times of our early youth, and played no part at all in the clothing of older brothers and sisters in the first decade of the century. Thrift and ingenuity combined were scarcely enough to keep us all warm and clean, and what was as important, respectable. 'I can't have you looking like speckle-birds,' Mother would say. Relatives did all they could to help, but the entire community was in peril, and lived only from hand-to-mouth. Parents put their children first, and when possible, grandparents, aunts and uncles passed on garments for immediate use, or for cutting down. Mrs Robins, Margaret's mother, was one of those specially skilled in the making of new from old clothes. There was no borrowing of money from outside, or having things on credit, and I don't ever remember a jumble sale.

Our shoes were worn quite thin, but well polished and constantly repaired sometimes at the cobbler's and often at home. We wore boots which buttoned at the side and socks and stockings hand-knitted. A cousin has told me how he once had a pair of boots made at John Beer's, the local cobbler's, but they didn't provide room for his toes, so that when he was called out from his seat at school, he fell over himself in agony, frantic in the knowledge that he just couldn't tell his poor mother. His feet would have to adapt to cruel circumstance until a younger brother could inherit the disaster.

Our outside coats were almost always made from adults' and so buttons were disproportionately large, and there was a deep hem to allow for growing. Our hats (rinkers) and scarves were of wool, done in garter-stitch. The hat turned up in a wide band, a working-class version of what is today high fashion, and advertised at inordinate prices from the best London stores. If ever anyone bought anything which wasn't good value, the judgement was 'They must have seen you coming!'

Patching and darning were so diligently practised as to become a fine art. Invisible darning in the fingers of gloves, and patching discreetly inserted into elbows, knees and tails. The irony of coloured patches imposed now as decoration on what are often very grubby garments, strikes me with such tremendous force, that I cannot suppress strong feelings of ridicule.

Mother and Dollie made most of our underwear, using

what I think was Aunt Carrie's machine. Dollie showed early promise at contriving, manoeuvring patterns and adapting ideas to little pieces of material which at first seemed hopelessly inadequate. Father's sister Harriet Louisa (Louie) worked with the gentry as lady's maid, and used to come home from afar with a box of ribbons, lace, buttons, remnants, bits of fur, and what Mother called 'fancy notions.' Not that she ever said as much to Aunt Louie, because she was too fond of 'that good-natured little soul'. Aunt once produced a pair of court-shoes for Marion, and she slopped about in them, her eyes glued to the ground in a transport of delight.

Then Aunt Etta, Father's sister who was connected with Seccombe's Drapery Stores in Cardiff, often brought home dresses and suits of her own for the older girls which needed very little altering. Already in their teens when I was an infant, they wore blouses with high necks, long full skirts and wide belts with a round buckle or a flower at the waist, their long hair piled up on their heads.

I remember a lot of Robin starch being used to stiffen our pinnies and underskirts, and there was always a horse in front of the fire full of bits drying for the next day. Unremitting, wearily unwearied, Mother subjected herself to an iron discipline, her face pale, her eyes watchfully anxious, her thin hands gnarled, she would screw up her face now and then and cry, 'Oh my poor feet'.

When we entered the twenties and moved to No 17, times improved, and clothes with them. We still had to be very careful and there could never be any waste. Marj and I had velour cloth coats cut down from Edith's and Marion's, mine in brown, and Marj's in kingfisher blue. On the back was a *fleur-de-lis* in fine stitching of the same colour. The narrow backs of the Junior garments incorporated a very much pruned version of the Bourbon arms, which we longed to conceal from the public. We used to stand with our backs to whatever wall was accessible, looking as unconcerned as we knew how.

The boys had navy-blue Guernseys, hand knitted and plain, in the traditional pattern. They were very becoming. Sail cloth jumpers in tan or navy, with a boat-neck were always made at

The Town Pump.

'Taching' the nets. Archie Lakeman,
Percy Behennah & Eddie Lakeman.

Mevagissey Regatta. Early Twentieth Century Luggers
leaving to race outside the harbour.

Dogfish posts with Mevagissey Parliament on the left

Inner Harbour showing *Ibis*, Fy. 119, at low tide

home. Similar garments hang now in Marine Stores and are 'affected' by women, old and young, who want to appear casually smart, and nautically up-to-date. I wonder what our mothers would say, were they able to examine the price-tags! Oilskins and sou'westers were a brilliant yellow, ordered home, and payed with oil before use. Sleeves were set in with a flat seam well down from the shoulder-line, into the magyar body, and hanging on canes, these oilskins swayed as they dried in the gentle breeze.

Sea-boots, made of leather and weighing several pounds came up to the thighs. They were made by local shoemakers, Alfie and Willie Whatty and John Beer and I never could imagine how on their thin legs the boys managed to carry them about. When actually fishing they lashed oilskin aprons over their oilskins proper, encased as they were then in armour as impregnable as that of medieval knights, but with surprisingly little of their amazing flexibility reduced thereby. True, they were thankful to remove all trappings when they came in, and especially the boots. We'd kneel down, we girls, and give a tug to the heel of the heavy boot and help drag it off. The oilskins often rubbed their wrists causing painful little boils, which they'd bathe in hot salted water. My father had very blue eyes and auburn hair, and his yellow oilskin and sou'wester were aesthetically just right.

Our clothes fell into three categories, best, second best, and working togs. Best suits lasted a very long time. When they began working the boys each had a best navy suit for which they were measured at Mr John Farran's or Whetter's of St Austell. They always wore white shirts, with ties according to taste, black shoes, and fine tweed caps flat on their heads. Eddie began tilting his cap sideways, and, lightly denting it with the fingers of his right hand, he'd come downstairs looking slightly sheepish. He also spent some of his 'uffy' (money paid for work before a proper wage was earned) on ties. These Dick would absentmindedly appropriate and wear, oblivious of owner, colour and pattern. Eddie was also the first one to break out and order a fine tailor-made suit from Stanley Prout's of St Austell, the local equivalent of Carnaby Street. He wore his best shoes on weekdays, and Marj would give them an extra clean, her infant hand lost in the cavity of the long foot. Then one day came an ultimatum. 'Eddie, I'm going to charge you for this.'

When we were on holiday in Stornoway in the early sixties, strolling through the town on a Sunday morning, we were suddenly startled by the emergence of a small army of men hurrying all in one direction, everyone in a navy suit. They were on their way to chapel, whither we too were making for the sake of old times. We had been shunted back half a century. Dick's suit now was dark grey, not quite right, but still suitably cut.

On Monday mornings Mother collected four best suits brushed them carefully, and aired them on the line before putting them away. Shoes were polished and put back in the cupboard. Except for weddings or funerals these suits wouldn't appear again until the following Sunday. Older men wore bowlers for best and trilbies for second best. Trilbies finally ousted bowlers.

Only the gentry wore top hats, and there weren't many of them. A popular brand of top-coat was a cross between raincoat and overcoat proper. Dun-coloured, its make was Sartor, and it had an almost eternal life taking on the shape of its owner so completely that it could very well have stood in for the live body in an emergency.

On occasions Mother would take one of us to Truro on Mr Willie Cloke's bus, a rare shopping excursion as exciting for her as for us. The bus first went to Gorran, and at the sight of Gorran Church Marj remembers exclaiming, 'Look Mother, see there, what a lovely cathedral that is.' Truro's most excellent drapery store Gill's occupied the premises now taken over by Woolworth's and was for us a wonderland.

There is still something left in Truro of the old obliging willingness and friendly intimacy. Assistants with comforting voices stayed in the same shops for a long lifetimes, serving their masters loyally, and the public with the same faithfulness. They were as ready to put you off buying an unsuitable article as encouraging about the purchase of, shall we say a hat somewhat outre, but right for your particular head and face.

Recently we were looking for an upholsterer's workshop in Truro, and entered the wrong premises. The proprietor came out with us, walked down the road, pointed out the place, told us it would be shut until 3 p.m. and then suggested a tea-shop round the corner where we could have a cup a' something while we waited.

We used never to visit Truro without going to Criddle and Smith's lost now in the anonymity of the House of Fraser. We were given personal attention savouring of gallantry. It might be a bedspread we needed. 'Right now let's see what there is. Here we are.' Expectation met with no disappointment and indefatigable gentlemen found time to stand back and survey with us any number of items, real works of art, laid out for inspection. You felt privileged to spend money there and got money's worth.

Before catching the bus home we'd enter the wide Post Office door and wait until someone fetched Marion. There'd be smiles and nods and greetings from Mr Lobb and others. It seemed such a vast important place equivalent to Westminster, a great institution with which it was almost an honour to be even remotely connected in a personal way on the lowest rungs of the hierarchy. That old granite Post Office opposite the Cathedral, has recently been demolished.

Shopping expeditions to Plymouth were few and far between, but did happen. There was a story about a man found washing his feet in a bowl before the fire one evening, and giving the reason as a trip to Plymouth the next day.

Once Marj with magisterial visions of grandeur asked Mother if she could possibly bring her home a white ermine fur. What came out of the box was a humble small brown animal with a bushy tail and a fawn satin lining, the mouth concealing the clasp. We learned very early never to be disappointed when dreams weren't realised, or at least to suppress regret, and make the best of what came.

Dollie found time after shopping, cooking, and cleaning to make dresses, suits and even coats. We used to send to Marshall and Snelgrove's and to Liberty's for patterns of Sale Materials, and when the fat package dropped on the mat we couldn't open it fast enough. Liberty's reduced silks and lawns filled us with rapture. Lightweight tweeds in subtle combinations of delicate colours made choice an agonising task. Voiles in pastel shades demanded quickly to be made into blouses. The order was finally completed; we were small, so yardage was kept down. Mother was prevailed on to choose a piece of silk which Miss Chivell of St Austell converted into a simple beautiful dress. Miss Chivell was an artist, equally good at cutting, fitting and finishing. Performing real service to the community, she brought great joy to many a humble respectable client. Her charges were moderate, her promises kept, and never was she even slightly afflicted by conceit.

Millinery was sometimes home-made as well, and this was Edith's domain. She covered shapes, pleating and gathering her materials, and decorating with ribbons in rosettes or streamers. One hat we always remember was a simple small brimmed shape covered in a Liberty's very fine woollen crepe in spider-web pattern of pale greens and yellows. It had a long streamer which fell on the shoulder. This was a Sunday School Anniversary special for Marj and went with an apple green velvet dress made by Dollie, pale yellow Star Sylko socks knitted by Mother, and black patent shoes with straps purchased at Lennard's. It was important to think out something different, and not copy anyone else.

My dress was of mole-coloured velvet with a cream lace collar not symmetrical, and having a small cerise ribbon bow attached. The hat was a wide brimmed cerise and cream coarse straw, with a plain cerise ribbon band: cream socks and the same black patent shoes completed the outfit.

Dollie's tour-de-force was a pale blue light weight tweed suit simple and elegant, worn with a white voile blouse. Shantung was very fashionable then and came in deep colours of turquoise and brown. I so loved one brown dress Dollie made for me that I patched the elbows in order to go on wearing it. Old clothes are a great comfort, and the stripping off of finery brings relief. Besides which Bunyan's Vanity Fair and its dangers were ever present with us, an important part of the theological background into which we somehow had to fit all our aesthetic propensities, our delight in colours, shapes and textures, and particularly personal adornment. Perhaps such tensions have their value for a more complex form of survival than obtains in carefree self-indulgent climates and in any case morality constantly needs re-defining in a world half of which is starving.

As for domestic fashions they were the usual Victorian with Cornish variations. Rope mats were common. Made at home by the men they were strong, thick and warm and kept clean by regular scrubbing in hot soapy water. We had several in our house white and fawn, hearthrugs and doormats. In a little book of memoirs I have read that 'from time immemorial in Mevagissey the abodes of the inhabitants have been proverbial for cleanliness without excepting the humble cottages of the fishermen.' Long cream or white lace curtains dressed the windows, fussier and fuller in some than in others matching the personalities.

I don't remember an interior that was uninviting: people loved their homes and took pride in them however small. Industry defeated inconvenience, and if poverty allowed of any taste at all, it was quiet and inoffensive.

Almost everyone was possessed of a mangle, and a high washing stool and wooden tray for the clothes. Water was heated in a furnace, and the 'copper' was lit on Monday mornings and later in the week for bathing. Galvanised tin baths hung on nails in the back yards. We used to bath in front of the copper fire in Tregoney Hill back kitchen, the little iron door left open and the red coals glowing. It was warm and cosy and clean.

Kitchens had white topped tables scrubbed regularly and worn smooth, and the best Cornish ranges brass handles, a brass top to the ash-tray and a lacy brass fender. Ours was cleaned once a week on the same day. Mother dressed up in her hessian wrapper, and did the flues, and then operated with black lead and Brasso. She worked like a demon, and got excellent results.

Feather beds were going out in the twenties, but I remember punching them and getting the feathers evened out. Some people refused ever to give them up.

Oil lamps lit the houses when we were children, and only slowly gave way to electricity which was too expensive to use freely. I remember the ominous crack of the glass chimney, and being given twopence to go up to Mr Way's for a new one. The brass lamp was carried around upstairs for a long time after electric lights operated on the ground floor only. Mother gave me her brass lamp in the thirties after I had begun teaching, and I used it in a farmhouse.

Almost every house had a couch in the parlour. They were often of mahogany, and covered in black shiny horsehair. We had one which stood against the wall and sometimes a hair escaped the cover and pricked you.

Stairs were covered in brown linoleum with a key pattern at the sides, and no dust ever settled on it.

Pictures were chiefly of rural scenes and gloomy, but in bedrooms texts were popular, with narrow frames of black ebony carved and crossed at the corners. I remember 'God is Love' surrounded by a mass of forget-me-nots.

We didn't have antimacassars in our house, but in some they abounded. At Granfer Pollards there were several in the parlour, red and green, tucked in and tidy.

We had crocheted doyleys for cake stands, crocheted mats for dressing tables and linen runners for sideboards.

Then there were those beautiful roomy cupboards you could stand up in, called spences. They had large blue stone slabs, and earthenware jars (stugs) stood on the floors. We had a very big one at Tregoney Hill, and I wish I had one now.

Television has familiarised everyone with many of these things, but to have lived and worked in a pre-technological age, and in a remote Cornish village is something different. Iron kettles have a sentimental value for the moderns, and inflated purses are opened to acquire them as ornaments. It was another thing to heave them about full of water, and to wait for that water to boil.

If we still feel that our days must always be filled with some sort of work that to rest for long is somehow unsafe even amoral, what wonder!

IX

Literature and Leisure

I faintly remember sitting round the fire on Sunday evenings while the older members of the family read aloud a verse each of some passage from the Bible. Not yet literate, I could only gaze and wonder and drink in the words. 'The Lord is my Shepherd' 'Who hath believed our report?' 'Hath the rain a father, or who hath begotten the drops of dew?' 'Blessed are the meek for they shall inherit the earth' 'Though he slay me, yet will I trust him' 'Vanity of vanities,' saith the preacher, 'all is vanity.' 'Where your treasure is there shall your heart be also,' 'The first heaven and the first earth were passed away and there was no more sea.'

The Bible was the chief of the few books we possessed, and we were each given a copy by Father when we were six years old. It provided us with stories, letters, songs, poems, history, ethics and philosophy. Through these various channels religion was conveyed to us, and politics deduced therefrom.

There is a great advantage in the whole of a society being acquainted with the same body of great literature. It provides a bond between the members, a starting point for discussion and argument, and collective enjoyment of the findings of men of genius.

That the Bible once fulfilled this function is indisputable, but at the same time it was the begetter of fear, superstition and bigotry. Our cousin Hartley Pollard has reminded me that at one time chains rattled somewhere behind the organ in chapel when hell was being described from the pulpit.

I am profoundly grateful to the Jews for the beautiful language and fine concepts they have bequeathed to us, but not so thankful for the confusion from which I have had to disentangle myself, nor the totally invalid claims that reason has had to reject. Drugged by brilliance, variety, beauty and false promises, and paralysed by the loud and often ugly voice of authority, one fails to see that the Bible can be a stumbling block on the road to truth. That morals should be identified with religion seems to me the most regrettable of misconceptions.

Next to the Bible came the hymns. Charles Wesley I discover wrote no fewer than *six* thousand. Rereading them, I find many to be tedious, morbid, and repetitive. Yet every now and then there are flashes of pure poetry which startle with their brilliance. One called 'Wrestling with the Angel' is in every line the cry of a sensitive, brave, clever and lovable human being, tortured with doubt as such a man was bound to be. It is too long to quote in full. The poet is seeking assurance that God is love, and as the poem proceeds he received the healing knowledge that this is so. These are the lines I come back to,

Thyself has called me by my name,
Look on thy hands and read it there!
But who I ask thee who art thou?
Tell me thy name and tell me now.

And in conclusion:

Contented now upon my thigh
I halt; till life's short journey end.

His prayer is answered, Doubt is dispelled. He is under what in another of his hymns he calls 'the shadow of a mighty Rock within a weary Land.'

We also made the acquaintance of George Herbert:

Thou has granted my request
Thou hast heard me
Thou didst note my working breast
Thou hast spar'd me.

and of William Cowper:

> God moves in a mysterious way
> His wonders to perform
> He plants his footsteps in the sea
> And rides upon the storm.

and of John Henry Newman:

> I was not ever thus, nor prayed that thou
> Shouldst lead me on
> O'er moor and fen, o'er crag and torrent
> Till the night is done
> And with the morn those Angel faces smile
> Which I have loved long since and lost awhile.

Moving slowly upstairs to change, Father would sing in a tuneless voice

> His name like sweet
> (Don't be long Father. No. All right)
> Per——fume shall rise
> With every morning sacrifice.

or from Isaac Watts:

> But saints are lovely in his sight
> He views his creatures with delight
> He sees their hope he knows their fear
> And looks and loves his image there.

He had reached the top of the second flight and we heard no more.

Third on the list of sacred literature was *Pilgrim's Progress*, and I am never despondent even now without feeling up to my neck in Bunyan's Slough. It was exciting to discover Maggie Tulliver's early acquaintance with the Devil. The incident made of her another sister, and further endeared her to us.

We inherited *Pilgrim's Progress* from Gramma Lakeman and

in the forties when the world took on such gruesome shapes as even at our gloomiest we had never envisaged, I re-read a good deal of it. Vision flashes across the page and the mind turns a somersault in instant recognition. Children love the abbreviated version as an exciting story.

We were given lives of the missionaries as Sunday School prizes, which we diligently read gleaning a harvest of geography and pluck. I have found one on our shelves presented to Marjorie in 1925; *Grenfell of Labrador*, published by S.W. Partridge, the author James Johnston, F.R.H.S. There are chapters on The Labrador Peninsula, Eskimo Race and Customs, The Fisher-folk of Labrador, and Romantic Sea-Voyages. Someone had chosen appropriately for us, particularly since we always approved of missionaries being doctors of medicine. In the first chapter I read of his 'commending the gospel with pills and plasters' and saying, 'If I were hungry and unable to support my family, I don't know any way in which the gospel could be better commended to me than through a chance to get fair returns for my labour.'

No wonder we liked him and read on.

The exploits of adventurous eager spirits, glad of a good reason to wander afar filled such books. *Women who have Worked and Won. Heroes of the Darkness.* Many of these Protestants, I like to think, must have pressed on with their backs to belief, looking over their shoulders perhaps, but making progress in doubt and fresh information.

One of our prizes was *Sense and Sensibility,* and when later we were able to tackle Jane Austen, this, since it was there on the shelf, was the first of her novels that we read. Out of Mevagissey Sunday School emerged Eleanor and Marianne, to be joined later by all the others of Jane's creating, familiar figures who walk about constantly in our heads.

From America we imported *Little Women* and *Good Wives, What Katy Did, Anne of Green Gables* and *Avonlea, Tom Sawyer* and *Huckleberry Finn, The Three Musketeers* and *The Last of the Mohicans.*

It has been most refreshing to see some of these stories revived for children on television, and to discover that the 'learnt-out' young aren't too sophisticated to respond.

In an article 'Riding down to Bangor' George Orwell calls up his own childhood pictures of America, one of New England, the other of the South, and I found such pleasure in agreeing with him about the enduring quality of these pictures that we conjure up from our youthful reading. For me Jo, Beth and Laurie are right at the heart of a permanent unalterable American scene and I can turn on Louisa M. Alcott and others so powerfully that Nixon and Watergate are completely blacked out.

A Peep Behind the Scenes provided our first incursion into the great wicked world of circuses. I believe there was a sweet unfortunate mother who died and an orphan girl whom weary cruel circumstances could neither weaken nor corrupt. I was greatly affected by it, and cried at every re-reading.

Angela Brazil wrote school stories full of smart prefects wearing ties who appeared in colour on the backs. We had *Playbox Annual* and *Girls' Own*. The pages were yellow with age, thick and spongy.

I loved *Tales from the Arabian Nights*, particularly Ali-Baba and the Forty Thieves, and Sindbad the Sailor. It is impossible ever to forget the magic of Open Sesame and the great rock rolling back. A passport to glory! I wonder do we ever quite outgrow the desire to possess such? As for Sindbad he always came out on top, and his largesse was quite magnificent. 'Here my good fellow take this bag of gold as a gift and let us be friends. Feel free to come and visit me whenever you wish.'

For the older ones it was an era of romantic novels, stemming from the line which Jane Austen satirised, and which is now continued in the highly-coloured paper-backs which proliferate on bookstalls and adorn the libraries. Mrs Roberts had a lending library at the post office and from that source there flowed the earls and countesses, colonels, sheikhs, French aristocracy, desperadoes and adventurers, and the willowy innocent beauties they seduced.

It was twopence a time to borrow, dearer than now; and as many as possible read the stories within a fortnight. They were consumed, passed round, recommended, highly or not so highly, and there was always a copy left lying about somewhere one could pick up.

I remember quite early laying hold of an Ethel M. Dell, and suddenly having the volume removed from over my shoulder by Arch. 'No more,' he said, constituting himself censor, 'that trash is no good for you.' He prided himself on sticking to Dickens and Scott. I found something else.

As for Mother, she absorbed the titles only, and sniffed. Once when the bread came back from the bakehouse sadly overdone she banged the bottom of the granite-like loaf, and shouted, 'Talk about The Rocks of Valpré. Tidden in it.' There was Baroness Orczy with *The Scarlet Pimpernel* and his *Return*, in a conspiracy to save as many from the guillotine as possible,and Marie Corelli with *The Sorrows of Satan*, though what they were I cannot specify. Rider Haggard's *She* cast a powerful spell, and there was a fine lady by the name of Beulah who gave her name as title to a book written by Augusta Evans, an American sentimentalist.

Beulah was a heavenly being with a very deep white brow whose fortunes everyone followed, but which I haven't retained.

Mrs Henry Wood's three volumes of *East Lynne* and as many comprising *The Channings* occupied half the population all the time. I learn that this prolific author was none other than the mother of the famous conductor, Sir Henry Wood.

Anthony Hope's *Prisoner of Zenda* and *Rupert of Hentzau* took us to Ruritania, and there was a satisfactory ending with the rightful heir landing up on the throne.

The two novels which stayed permanently on our shelf were *The Mill on the Floss*, and *Jane Eyre* left for us by Auntie Etta. Later there appeared *David Copperfield*, *The Old Curiosity Shop* and *Great Expectations*, because Arch became a Dickens' fan.

I made the acquaintance of Maggie Tulliver about 1923, and she has remained a close friend. There was no move of Maggie's with which I failed to identify. I hated everyone who was unkind to her. I defied her aunts, loved her poor father, and went along with alacrity to save Tom from the floods. Did ever such words evoke more powerful emotion than 'In their death they were not divided'?

Jane Eyre taking second place remains an important part of the literary experience of us all. Who better to supply us with the passion we so much enjoyed feeling than George Eliot and Charlotte Bronte? What greater release for the emotions could there have been than to hate Mr Brocklehurst and the Reeds, to love Bob Jakin, and take Dollie Winthrop to our hearts?

Later on I shared Thomas Hardy with my father who, released from heavy toil as the boys grew up, took to reading novels. He loved Quiller Couch's *The Splendid Spur*, the more so because it was written by someone so near, just up the coast. As for *Moby Dick*, it enthralled him.

Our two papers were the *Daily News*, and *The Children's Newspaper*, edited by Arthur Mee. Father spread the *Daily News* on the kitchen table and stood, bending over to read it, his battered hat pushed back on his head. He left Mevagissey and all other preoccupations for the House of Commons, and became so absorbed he was deaf and blind to everything that was going on. I remember the speeches of Lloyd George and Mr Asquith being read aloud, (Loud laughter. Hear Hear.) Isaac Foot was often quoted and held in high esteem. Then Mother would stand with the cloth over her arm, a resigned look on her face. 'Come on, Father, it's dinner time, I want to put the cloth down.'

'Yes, yes, Mother, of course, I'm sorry' and he retreated to the chair in the corner still reading aloud, and hoping for an interested audience. We took in quite a lot, and I have never been able to divorce politics from ethics from the life of every day, and the shape of the future of the human race.

As for *The Children's Newspaper*, we enjoyed it and read every word of it every week. I associate it with interesting bits of geography and history, little poems and biographies and conundrums. Once when I was sick, and reading nothing, I remember Father tiptoeing into my bedroom and laying *The Children's Newspaper* by my bed, confident that here was a positive cure for infection, depression, loss of appetite, the lot.

Ah yes, we wrung a great deal out of what might now appear as very little, and having savoured it well, we did what was equally important, we shared and discussed it.

The greater part of our recreation was incidental to work,

the pattern of working days being diversified by fragments of pleasure cropping up in what I always saw in my mind as the gentle decline of the week between one Sunday and the next.

All the luggers were moored up on Saturdays, winter and summer alike, and the harbour, empty in those days of pleasure boats, took on its Sabbath aspect of complete calm. God's discipline was visibly operating, and obedience patently shown to the higher powers.

Enforced rest was indeed a blessing to some of the fishermen, such as my own brothers for instance, who could easily have worked themselves to death if not commanded by God (or was it Moses?) to stop. The fleet looked like a congregation in itself, assembled in its cathedral with stout quays for walls, safe moorings as pews, the jetty for altar and the Sunday sky as roof, decorated sometimes with mackerel clouds or stained like church windows in deep rose-coloured hues.

We sang Lord's Day hymns:

Sweet is the day of sacred rest.
No mortal cares disturb my breast
O may my heart in tune be found
Like David's harp of solemn sound.

It must have been the very end of the twenties before we started to slip down for a bathe on Sunday afternoons, and then it was furtively. A few brave spirits like Jeanne and Nellie (Edwards) broke the bonds earlier. Walking was the thing, and you didn't change out of your best clothes.

However it wasn't too bad; we got a lot of fun out of chapel itself and Sunday visitors. Besides which we used to read a lot, and it was splendid not having to knit or sew.

A few abortive attempts were made by well-wishers over the years to organise our leisure time for us. Scouts and Guides never took on; we rebelled against imposed regularity, artificial situations, uniforms, and any suggestion of pretence. Private fantasies were all we needed. We went our individual ways and God knows being members of big families in hard times was discipline enough in itself.

As children we all roamed the cliffs, climbed the rocks, lay on the warm sand looking for shilly billies, fell overboard, were rescued at a tender age, and learned to swim very early with little or no tuition. The method was to throw you in to water not too deep, but not so shallow either.

Dr Grier had a tennis court, and a few of the better-off swung their rackets on summer evenings, the men in their cream flannels, the ladies in 'long shorts,' but I never saw a working man play tennis.

As for football, a less expensive pastime, the team flourished, though I think fishermen can only have been supply members, and the whole set-up was probably elastic enough to allow of absenteeism.

Dr Walker's daughter once came to our house on a Saturday morning to know if I would play in a Mevagissey hockey team. I refused outright. Time, free time, was precious in the same sense as life itself, and in any case I wouldn't have asked my mother for any money for games. I didn't tell her that though.

It is difficult to comprehend the almost complete obsession with sport that obtains now, and the vast sums that are paid to those who excel. It is I am sure a measure of the failure of our educational system which in turn reflects the hollowness of economic and political life. Essentials are subordinated to frills, and frills themselves become the raison d'être. Young people certainly need their sport, but so much of it proves there's a big empty gap somewhere in their heads. Like religion in the past, sport has now become the opium of the people.

We did quite a lot of walking, particularly in the winter. Father loved the country and we walked away from the sea, often to Kestle to see Aunt Murry. Marjorie and I both remember travelling through the thick mist, and being glad to hold Father's hand, and also the very place by the Coronation Seat where he explained to us what it meant to act with impunity. No punishment. Safe. Puzzling, With impunity. Without fear.

We had little lessons on the stars when skies were clear, and snatches of verse. 'The wind one morning sprang up from sleep, Saying now for a gallop, now for a leap,' and we watched the bare branches of great trees swaying eerily in the dark on the way home.

Our fantasies were chiefly related to travel, and we were installed in a well sprung pony jingle going to Caerhayes for a picnic. Dear Father. He was probably tired and longing to be on wheels, for he was not built for the very hard work which had always been his lot.

When we got older we sisters always went for a walk on the quays before going to bed – to the end of Island Quay first and then on the other arm to the Lighthouse. Little pockets of lights put us in touch with Looe and Polperro. Traffic in the Channel up and down, unceasing, brought the great world near, and we became sympathetic spectators of exciting mysterious communication on the paths of the seas. There was always someone walking on the quays whatever the hour or weather, and in the darkness we peered and recognised each other. 'Hullo, it's you. Wha'cheer. How be do'een? Fine evening (or looking poor) Goodnight. Goodnight.'

In the spring we went primrosing, a ritual we never failed to observe, as if we must honour the freshness, the delicacy, the promise of such a lovely flower. Later, just as A.E. Housman measured his lifetime in terms of the flowering cherry, so I came to reckon my own span of life in the number of times I should live to see the primrose reappear, and its pale face has for me a sad and precious quality.

On May 1st (Milk and Cream Day) when the weather permitted, we took a bottle of milk, and some splits and cream, and had our tea in some sheltered corner of a field. If it rained, Marj never defeated, used to spread the little feast on Mother's long tall, narrow washing stool, and invited a few friends to partake.

We picked elder flowers in early summer and the berries later on. The lacy flowers made poultices for ear and toothache, and the ripe berries went with apples into jelly.

We went blackberrying to Polsue and in the fields up from Cheesewarne and the Mill towards Heligan House. At Polsue the berries hung like a purple curtain, large juicy, and almost seedless, and a great silence fell as we lost each other in good spots. We trudged home, stained and scratched and weary, and as brown as bracken.

Every summer it was necessary to go to Hemmick, Ann Treneer's beach on the other side of Gorran. We took the bus to Gorran Church Town and walked from there returning in the late evening full of sun, and salt, and coastline, and wild flowers and distances to sleep a vaguely troubled sleep, still walking. How crazily prodigal, how splendidly indefatigable is youth.

Not long before she died, we took Edith to the Dodman, the great bluff headland up from Hemmick Beach, and gazing out over the summer sea to the Manacles she murmured, 'Look thy last on all things lovely.'

In January the boys went with us wooding. We seemed able then to gather wood without fear of trespass, dry twigs, stout sticks, and lichen-covered logs, all dragged home with determination. Pleasure was interwoven with necessity, work and play indistinguishable, and both mixed up with laughter, companionship and the crisp air of winter.

I must not forget the watercress from the Bottoms below Tregiskey, peppery and dark, filling up a white bowl on Tregoney Hill kitchen table with Vitamin C.

At the end of June we celebrated Feast Week when the children of every chapel were treated to a tea of a saffron bun, round, flat, buttery and full of currants, like a small cake. The festival is still observed.

Wesleyan Treat was always on a Wednesday afternoon, other denominations following on the Thursday and Friday.

We assembled in the Sunday School Yard, and lined up behind the band, a good one, perhaps St Dennis. Immediately behind the band came the banner held aloft on a stout pole by young stalwarts. Our banner was purple with gold fringes, and it had a splendid picture of Jesus blessing the children, 'For of such is the Kingdom of heaven.' Years before when he was young, Father had greatly exerted himself to collect enough money for the purchase of what he said should be a beautiful banner, and he always felt pride in its splendour.

White voile dresses and wide-brimmed straw hats were all the rage. We each carried a mug tied up in a large coloured handkerchief with a knot to hold on to.

Six beats on the drum and we were off. It was all too much for us; tears pricked the backs of our eyes. What glory, what happiness, what prodigious excitement! A lovely thing is a peaceful procession and the beat of friendly feet keeping time to rousing rhythmic music. The band led us through the narrow streets and out on to the quays, where we gathered in a small dense crowd, and sang, our Sunday School Anniversary hymns conducted by someone (Mrs Rowse?) standing on a fish box.

The streets and quays were empty then of visitors. We were the only important people on that day, and our praises, sweetly harmonised, ascended to the summer skies interrupted only by the squawking of a few gulls.

The one other march in which I have participated was in the fifties across Saltash Bridge in a C.N.D. procession carrying posters. I felt something of the same liberating loss of identity in a communal experience, but alas; we had no band, and indifferent cars whizzed by on lesser errands.

The singing over, our venue was the Lawn, the equivalent of a small field which stretched away in front of Treleaven Farm House, hidden amongst trees opposite the old Cemetery. The 'lawn' sloped very gently, the turf bright green and springy, and without hedge or fence, descended by terraces to the paths below. Trestle tables at the top end held all the cakes for the children, and on special ones with white cloths, was laid tea for the adults, cake and splits and cream. Darting figures fed the fire heating the water for tea, such tea too, served not from a tap, but from glazed earthenware teapots held in capable hands. From the spouts there rushed a hot strong brew to mingle with just enough creamy milk.

We ran around, up and down the terraces. A whistle blew, and the races began, three-legged, egg and spoon, and sack. We visited little stalls under the trees to spend any money we won, or had given us by friends and relatives. They were all there dressed up as fine as they could manage, in festival guise, a delightful colourful change from 'sacred' clothes. They sat at the tables and chatted, and the young ones were identified for those of the elderly who hadn't been out and about for a while. Anyone with a camera, then a rarity, used it, and performed the ritual of snapping.

The band played almost continuously, bursting forth with excellent items especially after tea. Gilbert and Sullivan featured largely in the selection.

Cap'n Eckey, the tenant of Treleaven, described by his grandson, my friend Jack Dunn, strolled round his estate, his chest plastered in medals, and a white peaked cap on his head. His bearing was as proud as if he were all the Squires of Cornwall rolled into one, and he moved grandly amongst the crowd, playing the dual role of public benefactor and patron of children.

Very graciously, at close of the proceedings, his pride controlled by affected nonchalance, he received from the superintendent the hearty vote of thanks he so much loved, and for which he had been waiting.

The band played again:

Abide with me
Fast falls the eventide.

Our gala day was ending, a sparkling splendid occasion full of sunshine and music of powerful emotions and indelible impressions. It was ending: it hadn't ended. Of course the fair had come, an intrusion from the great materialistic world, erected in the first field at the top of Second Hill. Mechanical music rang out over the high land, heterogeneous crowds licked ices and raised golden bottles to their laughing mouths, tents and gipsies, bare chests, gilded horses, and painted swing boats all merged in a maze of madness, and outside, the little black chimney of the chip-van smoked with fierce energy. Darkness was falling. The lights came on. The noisy mixture was all too much for my psychological digestion, and it was such a relief to see Father and Mother standing by the gate and to ask to be taken home. 'Yes, yes, straight now. You can soon be in bed.'

Feast week ended on the Saturday with an evening of sports in the outer harbour where great feats of diving were enacted and daring spirits balanced and progressed, or toppled and slid from a huge greasy pole. Crowds lined the quays and sat on the warm granite slabs of the lower part of the parapet while fleet-footed boys sped along the top, wild with excitement, crazily freed from every-day discipline. (Water-polo and the Floral Dance came years later, as entertainment for an increasing number of visitors.)

The band played again on the jetty, and the sweet strains had a plaintive sound now, as if carrying finality into the sky. There is a special quality about music over the sea.

The King's Arms, the Ship, and the Fountain filled up, and clocks registered Sunday morning. Silence fell on a community which would return to its sober Sabbath routine, and having praised God, get off on Monday to an early start at another year's work.

In the summer holidays on a Saturday afternoon we had our annual picnic in the *Ibis*. She drew up by the jetty, and was soon down-bends, not with pilchards this time but people, the family and its extensive ramifications of cousins and friends, all carrying bags of food. We packed ours in a flasket, which was a deep light clothes basket made of smooth fawn withes and having a strong handle at each side. These flaskets were locally made, and such a boon.

No need to take tea, teapot, cups, water or fire. The cuddy provided all such necessities. We towed the big punt, and landed at Trenarren or perhaps Pridmouth. It was the one occasion when Mother was always with us, still sitting bolt upright and with a look of delighted amazement upon her face. She never slumped.

I remember once the Pickens (our minister and his wife) being with us, and all the Dunns, Percy and Rosie too. We sat on a springy platform beneath the Blackhead where wild strawberries grew. Mr Picken was laughing, oh so gaily. The world was young.

It was as if the salt penetrated our skins, encrusted our eyes, and what a delightful weariness it is coming home on a boat from a picnic.

The *Ibis* was capacious, clean, comfortable and strong, chugging away across the bay towards the lighthouse, and it seemed impossible that any one of us could ever be a day older than we were just then in that moment of time, and more impossible still that we could ever be parted.

Polstreath was our Mecca, that long silvery beach on the north side half a mile from the village. It is approached along the coast from the battery by the Coastguard post, across a high field, and along a narrow path offering a descent in two places which we called the short and the long. You chose by the state of the path, treacherous or safe according to the severity or otherwise of the preceding winter.

Polstreath Cliffs are high, and to use a word of my mother's, verdant. Marguerite daisies, thrift, honeysuckle willow herb, bladderwort, wild rose and blackberry claim a habitat in different parts, and bracken turns the face into a golden expanse when the year declines.

If these cliffs had consciously decided to arrange their base for our convenience, they could not have obliged us more handsomely. Indentations offer small harbours which provide shelter and privacy, and we could always find a smooth perpendicular piece of rock as a support for our backs. Soft sand, diversified by small pebbles and thin blue stones, covers the beach. Ridges of rock enclosing seaweedy pools are exposed when the tide is low. It recedes so as to reveal two rocks in the centre, the cow and the calf, and when spring tides ebb the water round this pair is not more than a few inches deep. Flowing, it makes sure to rush everywhere, scouring the corners, so that we had a wholesome fresh terrain whereon to instal ourselves.

When we were young, Polstreath was our private estate, territory with which nature as patron had endowed us. No sovereign power, no feudal baron, no merchant prince was ever more solidly ensconced than we. Chance made us proprietors of a playground which the rich might have envied, had they been there to compete for its blessedness, a birthright entailed upon us in perpetuity.

We got up early, did a lot of work, Dollie made pasties, and off we went in the summer holidays, for the day. The pasties, well wrapped up were hot and juicy hours later.

We hadn't any beach-wear as such, except a bathing suit and sand shoes. If the sun beat down too fiercely, you put newspaper over your head. Summers were hotter in those days and you slipped in and out of the water drying in the shimmering sunshine. What water, clean, sparkling, still, transparent, warm, breaking lazily on the sand with the purr of a pleased cat, and holding what almost amounted to a conversation with you.

At the 'long' end a thin stream of water trickled down the cliff from the river above, bringing us fresh water for our tin kettle. We roamed the beach for bits of wood, a wonderful rewarding activity, and made a fire, in our spot. This operation was repeated in the afternoon. Nellie and Jeanne (Edwards) were often with us on Polstreath, loving the freedom and the particular beneficence of this our favourite haunt. We dozed after 'dinner,' but woke up as the heat lessened, and laughed and talked, seriously too. Jeanne's chuckle was the most infectious I have ever heard, and Nellie's firm judgements so full of good sense they could not be gainsaid. Dollie's comments were often the condiments of our feast of talk, but we all had a turn at contributing the main course.

When easterly wind stirred up the sea, and the still waters became violent and mountainous, we fought with the waves, seeking the treacherous level between one mighty breaker and the next. Marj remembers a great wave which, viciously full of pebbles and grit, hurled her up the beach right into the lap of Annie Husband who shrieked with fright. Annie was the fattest woman in Mevagissey and so Marj, bruised and shaken had found the softest possible resting place.

Mother didn't care for beaching, and on the very few occasions when she did accompany us, she sat watchfully with her hat on, and only shoes and stockings removed for a tentative paddle. She didn't trust the sea; it had caused her too much anxiety all her life.

The boys didn't go beaching either. They were always too busy, and would have only a quick swim in the harbour, diving off the quay.

There was a man who came to live in Mevagissey, one of the few early residents, who lodged with Mary Husband, and he practically lived on Polstreath. Bare except for a towel slung round his middle, he used to parade up and down the beach on the strip of wet sand left by the receding tide. Streakers must have descended directly from him. Mother was vastly amused by the boldness and stupidity of it, and derision fought with mirth in her face. 'What a *silly* man' she would say.

We loved Polstreath in the very late autumn just before winter storms began, and would wander there in the cool clear light, as if to keep company with a friend for as long as possible before having to part. I associate those autumns with the intense awareness of adolescence when the whole strange business of being alive strikes one with a force never again to be so emphatically repeated. There was one October Sunday when the wind was easterly, and Dollie and I found a warm spot by the archway rock on the 'long' side, lay down on the pebbles and fell asleep. On waking, I was acutely sensible of the sleep that would one day be death.

A stormy sea, and in the sun
The swift spray racing by,
Dancing and whirling, movement undying,
Only we shall die.

A blackened cliff and in the sky
A red sun sinking low,
Deathlessly noiselessly darkness returning,
Only mortals go.

Light in the morning, darkness at evening,
Sun on the sea and shade from the land,
Sparkling and speeding, spending and wasting
Lives like the sand.

When I was older I wandered on the beach quite alone in the January sunshine, and found inspiration of a different kind, a delight in winter as great as the joy of summer, and wrote in celebration of that memorable occasion,

If this be winter
Let the summer tarry long,
For the lonely beach is friendly and the
      salt air strong,
If this be cold,
Let the heat postpone its hour,
For the waters are aglow, and the rocks on fire.

If this be storm,
Let the raging never cease,
The cliffs are all alive and the full
      streams race.

If this be short
Let the years secrete their store
For this present has eternity upon its open door.

Years later we shared that beach with Paddington Green Evacuees, one of whom, Dorothy Elliott (now Kendall) was our own, and still is, for her parents were killed, and Gordon Gould, Arch's adopted, visits us from afar.

They had come to paradise, but near enough to the hell of Plymouth for us all to see the red glow of the flames in the sky. The frightened little mortals had gone through their Gethsemane, and rested now in the pocket of peace and security which Mevagissey, and Polstreath in particular had been destined to provide.

There remains Christmas, and I do not remember any community celebrations as such except for carols in chapel; those carols which recurred so mechanically. To my sorrow I have never received sympathy from anyone in my dislike of the rumbustious character of some of them. Only at the plaintive strains of 'In the bleak midwinter Frosty wind made moan' was my heart touched, and I find this little gem to have been the joint effort of Gustav Holst and Christina Rossetti.

I got a deal of pleasure sitting with my elbows on the kitchen table watching Mother and Dollie make puddings and cakes. Those were the only cookery lessons I have ever had, my Cordon Bleu complete, absorbed unconsciously while talking of other things and eating the odd raisin or bit of peel.

When Marj and I were in the Christmas stocking stage, our six brothers and sisters had passed well beyond it, and in consequence we were early disillusioned about the real identity of Father Christmas. Already uneasily aware of the truth, Marj remembers hearing Mother groan on the landing outside our bedroom door. On her way to bed, wearied with Christmas preparations she cried, 'Oh my dear life I haven't filled the cheeld's stocking.'

'This,' thought Marj to herself, 'is the end. I must tell Mother not to be bothered with it next year.'

Sometimes the boys went wild using the half filled stockings to give us a friendly clout, and we all suddenly joined in a game of derision of stockings so scantily packed and with only an orange and an apple to give them weight. In a sense we have played that game ever since, inimical as we are to pretence of any kind, and without expectation or indeed a desire for presents.

Once Marj's stocking got lost, but it turned up later in a cupboard, and we gleefully shared the contents savouring the taste of Christmas fruit in mid-January.

When we moved to 17 Tregoney Hill, the big room called for a party. Relatives and friends came and ate small beef pasties, ham sandwiches and mince pies. Aunt Susan and Mother sat together, near the fire, and contributed the alto to whatever songs or carols we sang, while I did my best on the St Ewe Rectory Piano, (German). How they loved to sing, and what sweet true voices they had. A rapt look stole over their faces while they nodded to the rhythms, lost to everything but the music, transported to another world, tenderly, thoughtfully happy and entirely free of self-consciousness.

We found an old fashioned dish in the sideboard, and filled it with nuts and muscatels to pass round. Nuts were cracked by the eaters, and we called Brazils pasty nuts, hard to crack like some people.

Hermia Lillicrap tells me that she was once present at a party, and met our cousin Ambrose whom she decided was of the very essence of Cornwall, fit to represent the county anywhere. Ambrose had a splendid voice, of the kind that makes you weep, and visitors to Mevagissey were always greatly impressed by it. In these days he'd probably have become a star, but I prefer to think of him as he was and is, friendly, witty, and obliging. He'd sing a song for you in the street if you asked him, and his chuckle is a mighty good sound to hear.

We played Consequences, and how sorry I am that those papers should ever have been destroyed; the lines reflecting their authors so perfectly. The consequences were full of the credibly incredible; the wit trenchant, without malice. I can see Edith's face still, alight with mischievous intensity, her pencil poised over the paper. So full she always was of invention and entertainment, fairly bursting with fun. Much more of it came out in the charades which followed; words had to contain not less than three syllables, so there were always four scenes. Nobody cared much about the word which got lost in fascination with the characters, and their improvised costumes.

Christmas passed. Winters were hard, and the sharpest part was to come. We felt reluctant to leave our feather beds to face the early start of the days. Parties receded, great gales blew, life was real and earnest, dangerous and desperate. Mother's face became pinched and anxious-looking, and often she was taking up her self-imposed watch at the high eastern window. The struggle was on again.

X

Some Characters

All essences in our village were quintessences, and strong ties of blood, triumphing over feuds, bound everyone together on a deep level particularly in the presence of 'strangers'. We must have been saved over the centuries by the occasional import of a Scottish husband, an Irish wife, a German immigrant, and by the sea bringing in a few foreigners. There was a host of nicknames. Lion, Boar, Squirrel, Buffalo, Topper, Black Eye, Sprat, Nango, U-fer-d-knaw, Shoeblack, Dandy, Ducka, Wakeham, Bonner, Old Dad, Sexton-Blake, Weesh, Ayshee, and Tenor-Hang-Out.

A traditional culture set pretty hard, making considerable demands on highly in-bred creatures facing what was in some respects an inexorable and inflexible code of conduct. Protest took amusing egregious shapes and there were so many eccentrics that the centre was left almost empty. Someone was always breaking out in an innocuous but highly individual fashion, and we had no need of a Roosevelt or a Churchill to grant us freedom of speech. No indeed.

The native population is reduced now to a few hundreds and universal fashion disguises almost completely what is left of the indigenous character.

An outstanding figure of our childhood was Cap'n Eckey, and Jack Dunn, his grandson, has described him and his career to me:

Cap'n Johnny Johns, grandfather of the Dunns, and famous diver began as a cabin-boy in his father's ship. Jack tells me he'd say to them, 'You ought to have had my father: he'd have killed 'ee well before breakfast.'

As captain of his own ship, the *Stirling*, he survived the great blizzard of 1891, and managed to bring his ship across the North Sea to the shelter of Beachy Head while scores of other vessels were lost. He finally settled down to farming at Treleaven, but as a farmer was no great shakes.

His nickname was Eckey, and once when a letter came to the P.O. addressed 'Mr Hickey, Mevagissey, Cornwall' (a 'furriner' who had only just arrived at Portmellon) Mr Jim Way, the postman tried delivering the letter at Treleaven. Nicknames of course were only used behind their owners' backs so when Cap'n Johns read the address he was mad with rage, and his language in consequence, unprintable! A form of migraine from which he suffered he called tic tolleroo, which Jack has translated as Tic Doloureux. He took enormous doses of pain killing drugs, enough, according to the doctor, to kill an elephant.

It was on Treleaven Lawn the Wesleyans held their feast under the patronage of Eckey, who, as I have described elsewhere, walked among the feasters, wearing his navy suit and white peaked cap. Adorned with his many life-saving medals he received thanks for the loan of the lawn, everybody crowding round to watch and hear his smiling acknowledgement of favour bestowed. Squire Tremayne couldn't have done half as well.

Johnny's diving prowess was widely practised and as well known. Once, in Sydney Harbour he earned the gratitude of a steamship company by diving repeatedly until he cleared a fouled propeller saving the company hundreds of pounds of demurrage.

There was also the time when Pentewan Dock Gates got jammed and harbour traffic was completely held up. It was Cap'n Johnny who finally cleared the obstruction. He always maintained that he once did the squire a good turn and so was promised he would never be turned out of Treleaven nor have his rent increased. Whether the 'good turn' was the work done on the Dock Gate, or saving the squire's life, his rent was never raised above the thirty or forty pounds a year that he agreed for.

His exhibition diving enlivened local regattas. He used to

dive they said with a lighted cigar in his mouth, staying under for minutes and coming up still puffing away at the cigar. Then he would dive with a bottle of whisky in his hand and come up with the bottle empty having drunk the whisky while under the water.

Farming incidents are scarcer, but there was an RSPCA medal once for a remarkable feat. One of the cows at Treleaven fell down a disused well and though neighbours came to help no solution was arrived at. Johnny then over sixty, was finally lowered down the well with a rope, and he dived under the cow and got the rope round it, so that it could be hauled to the top.

The other story concerns a ten-score porker which in 1922 Jack was to help his grandfather deliver at Polgooth.

Killed and scraped (what a job that was!) the pig hung from a beam whence it was lowered on to the butt cart and wrapped in pure white cloths. A butt cart was a kind of box on top of the shafts and wheels, kept in place by an iron pin. If the pin were not in place, there was nothing to stop the cart from tipping back off the wheels.

Johnny and the boy got up on to the plank over the pig. All went well until they came Perscuttle Bridge where they met inches of thick mud, and midway the road began to rise to meet the New Road not yet officially opened.

Then it happened. One minute they were riding along in the cart, the next lying flat on their backs in the mud with the pig on their chests. The cart towered above them kept in place by the pig while the pony galloped off with the shafts and wheels. Jack heard Johnny swear savagely and say something about that Jimmy who had left the pin out of the cart. He scrambled out and ran after the pony leaving the boy to get out of the cart as best he could. What a mess the pig was in. And to crown it all the rain began to fall in torrents.

Johnny found the pony at the foot of Vicarage Hill and brought it back. Just then Mr J. Coffin Rowe with one of his workmen came along and helped to get the pig down to the stream where they washed it off cloths and all, swathed it round and lifted it back on to the cart. They started off again for Polgooth (pin I imagine in place) and delivered the load.

Jack remembers his grandfather's incredulity when first he heard about Old Age Pensions and hears him saying 'Can ee believe it Jack? I shall have five shillings a week when I'm seventy'. The prospect was too wonderful to be taken seriously.

Cap'n Eckey was never wealthy, nor in any material sense prosperous, but when in 1934 he died, the West Country lost one of its most colourful characters.

Sam Rowe, musician, was equally renowned. A bachelor himself, he lived with his single brother Harry and sister Liza, the mother of Norman. Their father had been a very good blacksmith, and in early times they also ran a small bakehouse. The Rowes were poor, gifted very gentle folk, and Sam was particularly versatile. Dick, in one of his snap judgements gave me a good idea of the man. 'As for Sam,' he said, 'he could repair a watch with a 15 lb hammer.'

Liza had the sweetest voice imaginable. Perhaps she'd be waiting at the bakehouse for her tin of pasties and Mr Hicks (Johnny) would say 'Strike en up Liza.' Without affectation or importance she sang, and then just as sweetly, dear Liza smiled on the company.

Henry scraped a living by doing odd jobs here, there and everywhere. His was a sensitive spirit. He was taken ill on the quay and a small band of fishermen carried him home, very gently I'm sure. They laid him down, and calling Sam near him, Harry murmured, 'Sam, remember the boys.'

Their house was up the Lilley the next court above Myrtle, off the base of Polkirt Hill on the right, and a cul-de-sac. They were next-door neighbours of my father's single aunt and uncle, Elisabeth and Ferdinand Lakeman.

Now 'Ferdeen' was dying, and darkness falling, while Father sat by his uncle's bedside hoping to supply him with comfort. Through the open window there wafted the sound of sweet music, of voices mingling in perfect harmony, none other than those of the Rowe Trio next door. Ferdeen spoke. 'Richard, a heavenly host has come to bear me home. Can you hear it?' 'Yes, uncle, I can,' said Father. 'The angels are here.' Sam, Harry and Liza deputised for the celestial choir, and

Father saw to it that Ferdeen's splendid illusion became a blessed reality.

Sam played the cornet. He is reputed once to have walked clean over the jetty, when in a state of euphoria blowing hard on his cornet, he failed to look where he was going.

There was a P.S.A., Pleasant Sunday Afternoon Male Voice Choir which Sam conducted, and it met in the Wesleyan Sunday School after the children had departed. In he would come leisurely, shabby, plump, his waistcoat bursting at the buttons, his collar off white. Friendly dignity emanated from him. Hartley tells me he would wait with smiling patience for everyone to arrive and be ready, and then conducted with unflagging enthusiasm. What is more, he neither reproved nor dismissed anyone whose performance fell short of what he would have liked as a qualification for membership. Human values triumphed even over his great love of music.

Camborne Town Band was at that time taking National Prizes, and came one day on a friendly visit to Mevagissey. The conductor, good man, in recognition of Sam's gifts, passed the baton over to him, an imaginative gesture indeed, which no one could better have deserved than Sam Rowe.

He had a little humble property which he let, but never bothered to raise the rents from pre-war levels. There was a Music-room in that cottage up the Lilley, and it was very dusty.

Sam used to go to bed at 3 a.m. and rise at mid-day to breakfast on his lunch. One of his hobbies was the solving of knotty problems, which he tried out on anyone who was interested. He set a difficult one to Father, and was specially pleased, not so much at the correct answer, but with the method of working.

Passing by the Post Office on your left going towards the quays you will see on your right a block of buildings now occupied by boutiques of various kinds with modern flats above them. This was once a lofty cavernous marine engineer's workshop, the very heart of the harbour, regulating its life, and keeping its oily blood healthily flowing. A big door at each end stood wide open. Deeley Mann was the clever engineer who ran that workshop and William Hunkin, the late husband of Ruth Way, and a contemporary of mine, became his gifted apprentice.

Deeley had come from Wales, though I don't remember any Welsh accent. He was married to Edith, sister of John Farran, a very quiet unobtrusive lady, never seen on the quays. He had an eager, bright, large face surrounded by thinning auburn wavy hair; full of good humour he moved quickly and lightly. His figure was ample and square and his garb dark, shiny and oily. He delivered very correct English in a cultured voice, the sound of which, mingling with the Cornish dialect, made a pleasing alchemy of sound.

During the second decade of the century, engines, first Kelvins and then diesels, came to supplement sails, finally superseding them. Deeley, vastly interested in these developments, encouraged the enterprising and persuaded the prejudiced, of whom there were many, to adopt engines.

Mr Muirhead, an elderly man, came as the representative of the Kelvin firm, and stayed in Mevagissey for quite long periods, visiting Mr Mann daily, consulting with him and becoming a familiar figure in the workshop.

According to Dick, he was such a knowledgeable trusted member of the firm he could pretty well do what he liked. How lovely not always to have to refer something to a superior, but to make decisions and get on with it yourself.

Mr Muirhead was certainly no teetotaller, and when he lodged up at Windmills, one mile distant at the top of Tregoney Hill he pursued a zig-zag course home at a late hour.

The job itself however of well-equipping those luggers with good engines never suffered. With Deeley it was paramount, so much so, he had no time and less inclination to make out his bills. Father was constantly having to remind him of what he owed. He would bend over an engine with a Mark French's pasty (4d) in his hand, dropping it on any available surface when necessary. Food was an adjunct of survival, and Mark's pasties a very good fourpennyworth.

What a wonderful great living thriving place that workshop was, a world in itself of engines and oil, of figures flitting, of figures stationary, of great concentration and happy relaxation, of consultation and advice, of speculation and pronouncements, of repairs and renewals, of wit and satire, of repartee and reflection. I asked Dick who loved the place and learned so much there if he could sum it up for me. 'Well, Mary,' he said, 'it's difficult. We'll say BBC 2.'

Deeley had an old car, the only reliable part of which was the engine. He hadn't opportunity to use it until very late and then he would go off on midnight excursions taking with him Johnny Whatty the barber, a great friend. Johnny had also worked very late in his shop, and needed fresh air. They did moonlit tours of the coast, gay and reckless like hippies for a few hours off duty.

When his brother-in-law John Farran died Deeley attended the funeral in a very faded long frock-coat and top-hat neither of which had seen the light of day for years. Deeley's head must have expanded or the hat shrunk because the latter sat so uneasily that, had the cortège not been so slow, that hat would certainly have toppled and fallen. The mourner proceeded gingerly as if in a vice.

This was Deeley Mann, large and enlightened, the joy of all who came into contact with him, a human being to remember with affectionate gratitude.

A close friend of Deeley's was Frank Baron, the Cornish Bard, and Frank whose legs had never been helped by anything faster than a bicycle, took frequent outings with Deeley in the old car with the good engine.

Frank's nephew, John Baron of Truro, remembers standing on the jetty listening to Frank, Deeley and Howard Dunn talking together on historical matters. Would that even now we might overhear them.

Frank was one of a family of three brothers and two sisters born in Mevagissey and educated there.

When Frank was thirteen, his father died, and his mother who hailed from Truro took her children back to the Cathedral City. Frank, his schooling ended, became a grocer's apprentice, and went on to a managerial post in a jam factory owned by Sarah and Goodfellow. Always his employers sought his advice. It is a common mistake to suppose that poets and philosophers cannot be shrewd and practical.

The business was closed well before the slump of the early thirties which Frank in his wisdom foresaw. With the equivalent of a small pension, he turned his back on business and gave himself up to creative work.

Unlike any other Cornishmen of my acquaintance he and his brother Percy, a gifted artist, were Anglo-Catholics, and as a lay-reader Frank devoted much of his time to the life of St George's Church in Truro. Holidays he spent in Mevagissey, in his early teens walking the whole way.

He probably educated himself through correspondence courses, and began writing Cornish stories and verses. He lived with Percy and his family in Truro and the brothers did much in amateur dramatics, producing chiefly religious plays. Frank also lectured to the Old Cornwall Society. He was particularly interested in history and genealogy, and actually wrote a history of Mevagissey, where, his nephew tells me, his heart always nostalgically resided.

Language fascinated him and he sought out the subtleties of the Cornish idiom, achieving an unerring authenticity. I think of him as an amateur Quiller Couch in whom sophistication and naturalness blended in fine artistry.

Bishop Frere became conscious of the gifted man at St George's and offered ordination to Frank without the training that usually had to precede it. Frank refused the honour. He felt a strong distaste for hierarchies, and I am particularly proud of my countryman for that. He preferred to live and work among his fellows, for as a sincere believer, he wanted to follow exactly in the steps of his Master.

Frank was made lay-vicar of Indian Queens, the Mission Church of the Rector of St Columb where he worked for some years. During World War II he acted as Quarter-Master of the Home-Guard and let no-one think that in his earnestness he was without humour. Far from it.

After a breakdown he returned to Mevagissey and here in his real Home spent the last quite long period of his life. He had never married. First of all he lived with William Robins and his wife on their farm, and then came with them to their house high up near the Coastguard station. He was happy and stayed there until he died.

It was during this time I remember him, for he visited Mother, after Father died, and was always entertaining, friendly, amusing and splendidly courteous. Tall and quite handsome he dressed in tweeds, his plus-fours at first causing quite a sensation. How, being a rather shy man, he braved it out I don't know, but his nephew tells me he loved good clothes. When he came to see Mother he was wearing these beautiful nut-brown plus-fours, and as he got up to go, she said, 'Frank, you always did have lovely legs.' I can hear his chuckle now. It was just the sort of innocent uninhibited utterance he would appreciate.

His friendship with Deeley Mann is understandable. They both had the same intellectual curiosity and detachment from purely worldly affairs. Deeley's interest in engineering, in languages and people being matched by Frank's sense of history, of philosophy and poetry. They were both great communicators from positions of awareness which far outdistanced what is necessary for average survival. Considerate and undemanding, listening, observing, comprehending activists they were welcome wherever they appeared and missed sadly long after time had taken them away.

Now I see Tommy Whitford gliding through the front street in a black bowler, like an elongated shadow, dark, sombrely clad, and always wearing what we called sand-shoes, a speckly, as in a starling's feathers, plimsoll, adopted probably by reason of poverty and sore feet.

Tommy played many roles in the cause of a bare subsistence. One of these was to care-take at the Town Hall, where I have a vision of him standing in the door-way wildly staring, arms akimbo.

The site of the Town Hall half way up Church Street, parallel with and adjoining The Backlet is now a small Car Park. The building was not one to provide a background for a photograph of John Betjeman. A dark featureless erection, it wore an almost forbidding aspect.

I knew though, when recently I passed along by its old foundations, that it had once possessed a soul, and housed a lively joyous spirit developed over the years by being so obliging to the community.

From that shaky platform many an ardent election address was delivered in the musty atmosphere to a tense and passionate audience. Politics had a bit of substance in the old days. Bazaars revealed unsuspected skills and bred the usual rivalries; dances brought extraverts to the surface, and searched out the heavy-footed. Splendid cabbages and carrots appeared in horticultural shows with the mark of their growers upon them. Concerts and Variety Shows devised and acted by local artists entertained packed houses, and in later years the floor actually permitted of badminton.

In our young days Town Hall spelt PICTURES, and by that I mean film shows. These were provided on Saturdays by Jimmy Elgar, a suitably theatrical name you will agree, and Jimmy was further qualified to impress and succeed by the wearing of a fine waxed moustache.

His daughter Ruby (how I admired that glowing name) played a tinny piano quite relentlessly for hours: it stood perilously near the edge of the platform on the left hand side, and out of its innards Ruby extracted accompaniment for the tragedy, horror, romance and pathos that appeared in a series of jerks on the screen.

Dick says that Tommy Whitford would stand in the doorway trying to stem the tide as the children gathered in a crowd to enter, and remembers him shouting, 'Look out. My God. The Bolsheviks is rising.' His weapons then were abuse and sarcasm.

Marj never missed the pictures, and always managed to put back 2d to go. Once she tells me the head and shoulders of a glamorous beauty appeared above the rim of a bath filled with soap-suds, and as the lady, smiling broadly, passed slowly along the screen, the stamping, rhythmic and heavy, in which she joined was terrific. Sometimes the show had to be brought to a standstill because of bad behaviour and Tommy Whitford would appear, his long arms beating like flails crying, *'Less order please.'*

It's the piano I can never forget, that interminable music, with the force of an avalanche behind it, volume worthy of Beethoven himself. There were plays too like *Maria Marten and the Red Barn*, when the platform abounded in corpses.

Tommy operated in spheres other than the Town Hall. He worked the barge used for the cleaning up of the harbour and went out in the seine-boats entertaining visions of large catches which he was not successful in trapping. Swift-moving, excitable, unflagging, eternally optimistic Tommy remained a stranger to prosperity, yet an indispensable important member of the community.

Tom May who hailed from Port Isaac was the rag and bone man, and did some peddling in the district. Tom and his family lived up the Backlet, and Tom's accent, forged on the opposite coast had a foreign sound which incited banter. He lived as it were on the fringe of Mevagissey Society striking a provocative note of contrast.

Now Tom, peddling his wares, travelled to the neighbourhood in his 'dunkey' and cart. In those days vendors shouted descriptions of what they had to offer from the elevation of their vehicles. Jouters told the world of the varieties of fish available on any particular day in a language that no-one outside the area could possibly interpret.

Tom's cry was 'Pins and Needles, Brooms and Saucepans, Big Poes and Little Poes for the chill-drin.' How I wish I could get the intonations and rhythms of his cry on to this paper as I have heard it in the past from my brothers. I guarantee it would dispel the deepest depression into which any one of us could ever fall. Under Tom's mild exterior, his humble claims, his willingness to serve, his good-tempered disregard of ridicule, there resided a fund of philosophic resolution which special circumstance uncovered.

Tom was once a member of the crew on a schooner when a mighty storm arose, so violent that they all decided their end had come and resigned themselves to drowning. Tom disappeared below, and put on the frying pan.

'What's on, Tom?' above the howling wind.

'Supper. You can do what you like. I'm not go-in to 'eaven on an empty guts.'

Heaven on that occasion rejected a full one.

One of Tom's family was Abe, short I take it for Abraham. Abe was the great friend of John Arthur Thomas, brother of Adelaide. John Arthur, like so many of the Thomases had good looks and style. In World War I he practically encompassed the globe, and survived to describe his delight in the Arabs and their deserts, and his admiration of the Gurkhas. He would like to have been one of that splendid body in a remote romantic region.

John Arthur used to find a berth in this or that lugger, and having accumulated a bit of money set about spending it. He and Abe went off together, to Plymouth if funds were slender, or to London when the exchequer was fatter. John Arthur dressed up as a gentleman, very convincingly, and Abe as his valet, and when they entered the very best hotels in the capital, London's serving population rushed to oblige them. Indeed John Arthur was 'sirred' by head-waiters everywhere.

My brother Dick, who in all his life has never in my hearing boasted of anything, said to me recently, with a kind of shy pride, a sad reminiscent pleasure, 'John Arthur once told me that of all the boats in which he sailed he loved the *Ibis* best.' It would be impossible for anyone with any heart or understanding not to love and approve of John Arthur and Abe.

Steve Ball, brother of May, and Walter his musical son had a blacksmith's shop up the Backlet. Coming out of school as infants, our ears were assailed by a medley of sounds such as orchestras now make in the presentation of modern music, rather different from the strains which came from Myra's organ. (Myra was Steve's organist daughter.)

Steve's shop, warm and dry, was a haven in bad weather. The communication that flourished there was conducted in nods and winks to the clanging of the anvil and showers of sparks, the great bulk of a cart-horse claiming a good deal of the ground space. One or two would also be tied up outside.

Steve was once, in the very early days when times were bad, at a funeral with Father, and they arrived together at the house of the bereaved, for one of those 'feasts' put on by people who could afford it after the burial. 'Come on, Richard,' said Steve 'Now's your chance. Tuck in.' He wanted hunger to have its turn, and away with scruples. If Father were to eat up, well then so could Steve. I hope they both did, and enjoyed what there was. It is quite certain that they were pleased to be together, Steve supplying the fun.

Jules Toullec was the village photographer and had his studio under the cliff on the quay a little beyond the Lifeboat House. The tiny building seemed to grow out of the rock like a face, and has only recently been removed.

As a small boy Jules had come from France with his father, sent on a mission of instruction in the tinning of pilchards. When the time came for them to depart Jules was nowhere to be found, and the ship, along with his father, went without him, Jules reappeared to be adopted by Mrs. Jenkins who kept a bakehouse and loved children. Mrs. Jenkins also adopted Janie of whose origins and maiden name we have no knowledge.

Jules and Janie grew up together under the loving care of their foster-mother, and Janie went to school with my mother. It was a little Dame School they attended; the fee 4d per week and they did a lot of crochet. Mother learned to read and write, but practised neither after she married at twenty-seven, until her children grew up. Then she wrote every week to the absent ones, pages of lively English, badly punctuated, but with few spelling mistakes, and completely free of repetition or boring content.

Jules and Janie, thrown together by accident into the lap of Mrs. Jenkins never parted, for they got married, and went to live at Portmellon in the big house which stands where the slip reaches the beach. It was all black, perhaps tarred against the storms that have a good bash at Portmellon at least twice a year. I remember going in there and being entranced by an ancient, warm, shining interior, full of a sunny silence.

Janie remained a faithful friend to my mother throughout her life, and childless, came regularly to see Mary Sarah and her large family, but chiefly Mary Sarah. She had a slight impediment and spoke as if with a plum in her mouth. Edith knew how. At the bottom of Tregoney Hill, I remember gazing at her large placid face from which an unintelligible babbling proceeded, and then switching over to Mother's thin, alert, slightly sardonic countenance, across which there flashed gleams of genuine affection for her friend. They were single again, and they didn't talk about us, or bother with children during that pleasant half-hour.

Jules was a civilised mortal, courteous and proper, and keen on his photography during the practice of which he sometimes displayed the irascibility of the artist, or perhaps the continental temperament?

He once called Dick, Dollie and me (aged two) in from the quay, and co-opting Mr Bice photographed the four of us. Mr Bice was a carpenter, and father of Carrie, one of the very first to gain a scholarship to St Austell County School. I have seen pictures framed by Mr Bice.

The inside of Jules's Studio abounded in paraphernalia of all kinds, material for whatever décor he chose. There was a heap of backcloths, probably old counterpanes, and the odd cane which you were given to hold at any angle.

Jules disappeared under his ample hood for what seemed an eternity, during which time the agony of suspense played havoc with facial and abdominal nerves, causing twitching without and hysteria within. Marjorie and I were taken together in 1918, and I came out bearing down on my cane with shoulders hunched up to my ears in response to a feeling that the lace of of my drawers was showing. My sober face reflects acute anxiety.

Later on when times were good, we had a family group taken by Jules, and Cap'n Pollard offered his lawn fringed with palms as a background. We all trooped up the hill and must have been there for at least two hours. Jules retreated under his hood, and whenever arrangement, light, and expression were satisfactory, somebody, probably Dick, made a remark (sotto voce) which caused a strong ripple of mirth to pass through the set, the vibrations disturbing everyone except Father, who sat impassive, full of a great concern for Jules.

Jules's patience began to run out, irascibility took over, and Father's displeasure mounted. 'I'm ashamed, ashamed,' was the equivalent of powerful censure.

Our photograph wasn't a success, for expressions were all unnaturally sober or silly, reflecting the duress which had been afflicting us.

In early times Billy Fulfit was the Town Crier, and not long ago, his grand-daughters came from America to Mevagissey seeking out those who had known their Grandfather.

Billie, very tall, pale and slight had a white beard, and bending over to his task through long dedicated years he had become almost concave. Equipped by nature with a stentorian voice, and managing his handbell with skill, like others of his kind he sired the BBC. Maybe some of his broadcasting progeny have not even yet surpassed him.

The most frequent of his cries was LOST, at which everybody pricked up an ear. 'BETWEEN PORTMELLON AND POST (as in lost) FRIDAY NIGHT A DIMOND BRAUCH.' Now Billie was on tiptoe, and second ears were alerted at 'REWARD OFFERED'.

Billie read out details from a piece of paper held aloft in his free hand, for like so many of his 'uneducated' contemporaries, he was literate. What good children they must have been. I am told that the WELSH MAIDS came from mountain fastnesses to sing to their Cornish cousins, and it was Billie's privilege to announce their arrival.

Everything offered by the Town Hall, politics, sales, concerts, shows, pictures, dances, it was Billie's business to make public.

What a splendid occupation to be society's prime communicator, to enlighten and forewarn, to bear interesting tidings, to dispense welcome diversions, to shatter weary monotony, and defeat uneventful days.

Billie mattered, and gave his lungs to the community.

Randolph Fulfit must have been called after a Churchill, and certainly possessed, whether or not by virtue of his name I couldn't say, some of the characteristics of that family. Could he have afforded cigars he'd have smoked them with a Winstonian effrontery.

He was a short man, very excitable, wore a floppy wide brimmed hat and his wide trousers always seemed to be falling down, the waist insecurely residing on his hips inside a loose leather belt. He should have owned a log-cabin.

One of his utterances became common coin, and we still use it whenever we feel oppressed by our betters. 'I'll have no boss under me.'

Randolph was a master at conveying what he meant in sentences without any sense in them. 'I doo'an put my hand in front of anybody's back' was intended to warn his audience of the dangers of disparaging him.

Willie Williams matched Randolph for excitability, loquacity, swift movement, and being everywhere at once. They were essentially dramatic those two, but in other respects unlike. Willie was tall, smart and fastidious. He lived in the old house next to the Mill Wheel and glided in and out of the Mill opening, his tall body swathed in pure white, his feet turned out, and his mouth full of words.

When work was finished and he tidied up, he was a regular swank, wearing lemon gloves and shining shoes. He used to called our Eddie, one of the crowd of boys who teased him, the great actor, but he was a greater one himself. What a romantic corner that was, the old Mill Wheel covered in lichens, the gentle stream running below, Willie's house exuding flour, and Grannie Craggs up over looking out of her window. The buildings there now include a bank of all things. Passing by, and remembering I feel as dismayed as if I were being forced to work as a bank clerk.

Willie's place, very central was a rendezvous for the wits, like Mrs Beswarick, Tilly Williams, and Lily Barron. Tilly had a graceful figure, and very mobile features which worked as hard as that of her namesake Kenneth. Country folk waiting for the bus would drop in there, like the Polmassick woman with a very plain face, and a clumsy new denture, the latter described by Tilly as 'a passel of sherds'.

Howard Dunn, who appears in my account of school and chapel, died in the thirties not long before Father. Incredulous and sorrowful, I watched his funeral procession pass down Polkirt Hill. Howard, gone. He was built for immortality.

A man of substance, fishbuyer, county councillor, handsome and daring, he lived in the white house at the top of Polkirt Hill, a residence which suited his status.

As Chairman of the Harbour Board, he despatched business with justice, good sense, and expedition. There was no greater democrat than he. More money, and some education did not remove him from the fishermen, among whom, non-patronising, he moved freely every day, taking an active part in public life generally.

Irreligious, swearing and cursing with impunity, and without malice, he made a splendid bastion against humbug.

He had academic aspirations, and appeared at our Wesley Guild to give papers, his great love being ancient history, the first rather unbalanced dose of which I received from him in our Sunday School. You had to listen to him, his personality was so powerful, but it was hard to desist from helping him out with a word or two now and then. I believe under all that bravado of his, he may have been nervous.

I am glad that his reforming, liberal spirit was not daunted in old age by the horrors of World War II, that he died believing in progress, with hope in his heart, his concern for the young undiminished and a great love for his native village unimpaired.

A few years ago Albert Hunkin died, and when his life ended I imagine the faces of the houses encircling the harbour to be wearing a look of regret. Dick walked in and out absently, and without speaking for several days.

The essence of our small community settled very strongly in Albert and if you saw him leaning over the wall on the Cliff Side talking to a pal, you knew that some original communication was being made.

Once, in her teens, Marj decided to go pilchard driving for a night in the *Ibis*, and in the early morning our boat drew up at the steps beneath the lighthouse alongside Albert. Chipped by Dick, he kept up a constant almost one-sided stream of talk while the small catch was being landed. Then he shouted, 'For goodness sake Dick, stop yer ole chattereen, and give the maid a chance to git ashure. She's tired.'

At Deeley Mann's workshop he made a request to William for something or other, and William, intrigued and amused by the specification, asked Albert to repeat what it was he required. 'Look here, William,' said Albert, 'never you mind what I'm asking for, you give me what I want.'

Primuses became popular for the boiling of kettles on the boats and, wearing an eager rapt look, Albert said that a cup a'tea out the primus was a fine thing.

His friend Percy, younger and obliging, accompanied

Albert to St Austell to collect his first unemployment card. That word *Dole* carried strange echoes, alluring and repelling, and Albert had grave doubts about the legitimacy of drawing unemployment money. Percy described the scene of Albert confronted by the clerk.

'Who are you, my man?'

'Albert, Albert Hunkeen. Yes that's right.'

'And who do you work for?'

'Willie, wey Willie, Willie Frazier.' (Willie was his boat-builder father-in-law)

'How much do you earn?'

'Well now, a few shilleens.'

'Only a few shillings?'

''Es, a few shilleens, or there, perhaps a bit more sometimes.'

'That's all right, Mr Hunkin. Here's your card.'

Albert had a way of dwarfing anyone with pretensions, and inoffensively dismissed by his chuckle whatever was specious.

Percy, son of Verinder Hunkin, was one of Mevagissey's most intrepid, intelligent fishermen, as unassuming as he was capable. When a little boy, he was sent with a big white jug for milk, and passing through the Greenfield encountered a cow belligerent on behalf of her calf. Percy ran away, but, having got beyond reach, decided he must return and confront the animal. He approached her, broke the milk-jug on her head and went back to his mother, who without any comment, gave him another jug. He grew up to be the most valiant member of the lifeboat crew. With Percy there, they shed their fears, and trusted to him to see them through.

When he was nineteen his father died, and the boy took charge of the *Vesta*, their lugger, and worked her successfully. He married Rosie, daughter of Billie Blamey, the harbourmaster, and their eldest child was a son, Alec. Alec began to wander on beach and cliff as soon as he could walk, and at five years was in Pentewan on the Winnick searching for his uncle. He climbed over to Portgiskey, was cut off by the tide and drowned. Percy and Rosie had three daughters and then years afterwards another little boy Lloyd, who came to take Alec's place.

Percy's crew was ageing, and he could no longer continue to work the *Vesta*, so he came on to the *Ibis*, where he stayed for many years as the trusted friend and partner of my father and brothers. There was a strong bond between them, and the *Ibis* the best substitute for his own boat which he could have found. Ten years senior to Dick, he became an older son to our father, and a brother to the boys. Rosie is still alive, and in Plymouth. She loves to remember.

One day, as the boat was entering the harbour, Olive's husband, Percy's son-in-law stood solitary on the quay. He was waiting to tell Percy of a calamity too incredibly terrible to contemplate. The second little boy Lloyd had fallen from a high cliff and was dead.

There was the day when Mevagissey fishermen went to St Ives for the funeral of the members of St Ives lifeboat all of whom had been drowned. They should never have put to sea. One of their members had said the venture was mad, and decided to withdraw. I remember the boys with Percy and Ambrose and Willie Husband setting off for St Ives. It was crushing, too much for the heart to bear. On that occasion Dick asked Percy, whether, had he been of St Ives Crew, he would have ventured, for Percy more than anyone could have judged the possibility of survival. 'Yes, Dick,' he said, 'I'd have gone.' He was as empty of false modesty as he was of conceit.

I see Percy's face so clearly, bronzed, long, lean and keen, framed in thin curling hair, and a shy far away look in his eyes. His figure was slight, and he wasn't very tall. He has been dead these fifteen years. Of all their faces I have written:

Stormy experience
Stamped on the features
Lifetimes of struggle
Mapped in bold tracery
Patterns significant
Certain and sure.

Flood tides of confidence
Ebbing endeavour

Fair winds of triumph
Fierce rains of failure
Mists of bewilderment
Defiance, despair.

Slow transmutations
Fear become courage,
Hope, resignation
Ambition, acceptance
The present, the future
The future, the past.

Far distant horizons
Visions magnificent
Private discoveries
Gleams of infinity
Cerebral journeys
Trapped in the eyes.

Nature's cartography
All authenticity
Perfect ecology
Script in the flesh
Fashioned distinctively
Consummate skill.

It is during this August of 1977 that I have read with great appreciation a review of John Dyson's *The Price of Fish*. The author we are told makes the observation that the fishermen's faces are not such as you would see on a committee. They belong to men who, as rugged individualists go their own way, and too often sometimes for their own good. How true, and with what readiness do I, as a fisherman's daughter confirm what the reviewer says about this 'romantic occupation enviable to the deskbound, and the reality which is more often a dark shade of nightmare'.

The other Percy, a contemporary of Dick's was ten years younger, and died in 1970. He was Percy Mitchell and married Enid Pollard our cousin, daughter of Uncle Ambrose. Percy appears as one of *A Hundred Famous Cornishmen* recently published.

His own book *A Boatbuilder's Story* is as moving as the publishers claim it to be. We all knew what courage, initiative, ingenuity and patience he possessed, but it is the sheer bulk and variety of his achievement which comes out in the book and is so amazing. The boy had had no tuition whatever in designing, but had put together such information as he found in his father's encyclopaedias. During long years of unremitting, unostentatious dedication to the job he loved, Percy's great talent emerged to take on a look of genius, and he became famous in boatbuilding circles throughout the country.

His style is terse, and in real life his silences were more eloquent than his speech, but he could be very droll, and perceptive about much more than boats. He loved his music, and painted in oils choosing always the sea and ships as his subject. In Eddie's house is a painting by Percy of the *Ibis* FY 119. Having built her, he put her on canvas, and amidst a blaze of colour, she moves on the sea with the same pride as he had felt in her construction.

Percy had great difficulties with launching his craft at Portmellon on several occasions. Less dogged, more timid spirits would have been daunted by hearing 'Mitchell is building av'er but e'll never git 'er in the watter.'

He tells of how it was in chapel, that he found answers to his problems.

While the sermon was being preached, it came to me how the job was to be done. (no reflections on the preacher.) – it was planned in the Congregational Chapel during Morning Service. The method was as clear as daylight. If you would care to come to Portmellon you can see for yourself what a simple arrangement it is.*

When Percy and Enid were entertained at Carlyon Bay Percy tells how the thought of his Uncle Johnny who went out to a post office dinner with hs son George in Bristol. There was an 'imposing array' of knives and forks and after dinner George said,

A Boatbuilder's Story published by Kingston Press, Mevagissey.

'How did you get on then, Father?'

'Well now,' said Uncle Johnny, 'I watched everything that you did, and I would count two beats, and then I would do the same, and if you had ate your serviette I would 'ave ate mine.'

It looks as if Uncle Johnny and Percy were endowed with the same uncommon powers of observation.

Percy was religious in an untheological flexible way, a member of the Congregational Church. He taught in Sunday School, sang in the choir and during the war took on the duties of Church Secretary and Sunday School Superintendent. It was a pity he did not live to enjoy a long retirement, for he could have filled every day with interesting pursuits, and the community would have been that much richer for a little longer.

The wall on the cliffside overlooking the harbour and facing south is old, smooth, and saturated with heat.

Imagine two figures, one slight, the other stocky, like the sculptured ones in Gift Shops, leaning over that wall. They are the cousins Dick Lakeman and Ambrose (Amburze) Pollard, both in their seventies and alive now in 1977. They are wearing navy jerseys and dark trousers.

There is a great quietness locked up in those bodies, a stillness as still as the wall itself; it belies the activity behind their eyes, one pair blue, the other brown. Trained to observation from birth, they are scanning every object, every movement on land, sea and sky within range of vision.

Gazing straight ahead, Dick speaks to Amburze in low tones. A few moments elapse. Amburze replies. What they have said the world will never know.

They turn towards each other simultaneously, eyes sparkling, and with grins stretched right across their brown seamed faces.

They part in different directions, heads down, and with chuckles that come from deep down in their bellies.

This is the essence of the life that I have tried to capture, elusive, subtle, rich in a kind of alchemy ever at work to turn out something new from elements that lend themselves to a billion combinations.